CONVENTIONAL DEFENSE AND TOTAL DETERRENCE

CONVENTIONAL DEFENSE AND TOTAL DETERRENCE

Assessing NATO's Strategic Options

WITHDRAWN

Robert B. Killebrew

SR *Scholarly Resources Inc.*
104 Greenhill Avenue · Wilmington, Delaware 19805-1897

The paper used in this publication meets the minimum requirements of the American National Standard for permanence of paper for printed library materials, Z39.48, 1984.

UA
646.3
.K476
1986

© 1986 by Robert B. Killebrew
All rights reserved
First published 1986
Printed and bound in the United States of America

Scholarly Resources Inc.
104 Greenhill Avenue
Wilmington, Delaware 19805-1897

Library of Congress Cataloging in Publication Data

Killebrew, Robert B., 1943–
  Conventional defense and total deterrence.

  Bibliography: p.
  Includes index.
  1. North Atlantic Treaty Organization—Armed Forces.
2. Europe—Defenses. 3. Warfare, Conventional.
I. Title.
UA646.3.K476   1985   355.0215   85-19612
ISBN 0-8420-2248-1

For My Comrades

Contents

List of Illustrations, ix

Preface, xi

CHAPTER ONE
Conventional Defense, 1

CHAPTER TWO
NATO's Central Front, 21

CHAPTER THREE
The Soviets and the Warsaw Pact, 55

CHAPTER FOUR
Surprise and Mobilization, 85

CHAPTER FIVE
Realigning Conventional Strategy, 113

CHAPTER SIX
Finding the Right Questions, 141

Selected Bibliography, 149

Index, 155

List of Illustrations

Maps

1. Three Pact Avenues of Attack 23
2. Corps Sectors in NATO 39
3. Soviet Theaters 71
4. Built-up Areas in West Germany 106
5. Recommended Corps Sectors in NATO 119

Tables

1. Selected European Reserve Establishments 51
2. Estimated Rates of Growth of Soviet GNP and Selected Subdivisions 59
3. East European Reliability in a Warsaw Pact Attack on NATO 77
4. The Non-Soviet Central Front Powers 78
5. NATO and Warsaw Pact Ground Forces at M+14 101
6. NATO and Pact Aircraft Reinforcement 103

Diagrams

1. Breakthrough Attack Deployments (Tank Units): Soviet Echelonment Concept 63
2. NATO Combat Units and Soviet Forces on the Central Front 105

Chart

Shifting Warsaw Pact/NATO Force Balance in 1980: Ninety Days Following Pact Mobilization 117

Preface

NOT MANY SERVING military officers have the opportunity to reflect broadly on military philosophy and strategy since the mechanics of our business are intensely practical and direct. Our professional model is more like Frederick the Great, who was forever concerned about the shoes of his troops, or Nelson the close-in fighter, than theorists like Clausewitz or Mahan. I was fortunate to spend one year as a student at the Naval War College, in Newport, Rhode Island, and then a second year as Visiting Defense Fellow at Queen's University, Kingston, Canada. That time to study, in the company of a number of exceptional people, led to this book.

The United States and the world have entered into a period of profound historic change, a kind of interval between the tectonic plates of historical eras. Perhaps the closest analogy would be that time between the breakdown of the feudal system and the rise of European nation-states. The delayed impact of two calamitous world wars, the breakup of colonialism, and the technological revolution are sweeping us toward the twenty-first century and an uncertain world order, in which the application of military power is liable to be very different than it has been in the familiar past.

General André Beaufre, in his *Introduction to Strategy*, has remarked that strategy is only the operational concept of a society's philosophy. A military strategy, based solely on tactics and operations and planned in a political and social vacuum, is ultimately a house of cards. Certainly the U.S. operations in Vietnam were tactically and operationally superior and our forces more proficient and better supplied. Equally certain, as a North Vietnamese colonel observed, that was irrelevant. For the foreseeable future the United States is going to be contending with deadly adversaries in an increasingly dangerous world, as the world's peoples go through this historic period of readjustment. We need, and must have, a philosophy and national strategy for the use of force, one that will knit together the rifleman on the point, our command structure and government, and the people themselves.

A "philosophy" for the United States is a little high-sounding; we are a conspicuously unphilosophical nation. We will fight for ideals (we have not gained one inch of soil for ourselves in our four major wars of this century), but once in we expect success. Perhaps our single most consistent philosophy is that we want our efforts to "pay." Both Korean and Vietnamese battlefields failed to produce success, and the national will rebelled.

Our national strategy for the coming decades, then, must at least hold out the prospect of success in whatever conflict is being discussed. Military philosophers may debate the meaning of "success," but to the American people it means emerging as a clear winner in a contest of arms, either by holding the battlefield, or by destroying the enemy, or both. A national strategy that plans for a draw, with the possible exception of nuclear weapons, flies in the face of our expectations as a people.

This is the issue regarding our support of NATO strategy today. To a growing segment of the American public, the Alliance's present reliance on nuclear weapons does not pay. Unless we loosen our dependence on nuclear weapons, or more specifically on mutual destruction, we ultimately stand to lose public support for defense. This is the appeal of President Ronald Reagan's Strategic Defense Initiative ("Star Wars"). Freeman Dyson has said the same thing in *Weapons and Hope*. Whether one agrees completely with Dyson, and this author does not, we cannot dodge the fact that nuclear weapons have led us to a strategic dead end. It is the task of military professionals, among others, to find a way out.

That a Soviet or Warsaw Pact invasion of West Germany is an unlikely contingency does not mitigate the fact that, after defense of the continental United States itself, the defense of NATO is our most serious commitment. Protecting Western Europe is at present the keystone of the U.S. defense effort. While we are more liable to commit forces elsewhere in a lower-intensity conflict, we must be able to articulate a coherent overall defense strategy that reflects our priorities and makes sense to our constituency. Clearly, continued defense of NATO, and deterrence of a war in Europe, are vital to U.S. national military strategy. To produce a strategy that is acceptable to our people over the long haul, we need to find a way to deter war in Western Europe, thereby offering an alternative to nuclear stalemate or worse.

Thinking through strategic problems is never easy since so many diverse issues are involved, some of which initially appear substantial but later become irrelevant on closer examination. The question of "no first use" is one such case; the maritime and continental strategic debate is another and is addressed in the following study. It may be that the evolution of sound U.S. military strategy will require the reorganization of the country's defense apparatus, as Keith Dunn and William Staudenmaier have concluded in *Strategic Implications of the Continental-Maritime Debate*—and I agree. Military reform, however, is a separate issue from the theme of this study which focuses somewhat narrowly on a strategy for the conventional defense of NATO.

This book would not have been possible without the support and help of many patient people, whose roles I gratefully would like to acknowledge. First, my heartfelt thanks must go to the U.S. Army for giving me the chance to pursue this study and for the support I received from so many of my fellow soldiers and civilian employees.

I am indebted as well to the Fellows and staff at the Queen's University Center for International Relations for their support and intellectual honesty. Especially I must acknowledge a debt to Nils Ørvik, then director of the center. Nils is a former World War II Norwegian resistance fighter, a scrappy, uncompromising Viking whose dedication to the ideals of Western democracy has led him through a strenuous life in academia. He is a true champion of freedom. His periodic raids on my manuscript kept me generally in line, and I treasure his friendship.

At the Naval War College, Lieutenant Colonel (ret.) Bud Hay, USMC, and John Bird were constant friends and counselors during the past two years. As a relatively junior officer, Bud guided and executed at the Naval War College a series of far-reaching analyses of defense strategy. John's penetrating intellect and his impatience with hidebound thinking kept me on my toes. Together, they taught me to look for the right questions, and this study has profited immensely from their programs and support. The defense bureaucracy is so vast that the true extent of their contributions will never surface, but Bud and John are leading figures in the real "defense reform" movement going on within the services today, and the nation owes them a great debt. I owe them my heartfelt thanks for their help and fellowship. Colonel Lee Briggs, USA, was at the time a member of the faculty and an authority on NATO logistics and deployment. He was my army "base" in a world of sailors and marines, and his friendly counsel helped immeasurably.

At the Army War College, Colonel William O. Staudenmaier and his associate, Keith A. Dunn (now of the National Defense University), gave me support and advice throughout the study. They continue as associates, and I am honored by their friendship.

This work would never have been attempted without the support and understanding of my wife Pixie and daughter Elizabeth. They have just finished their nineteenth move in eighteen years, and Elizabeth the fourth high school. For the moves, the constant separations, the copyreading at midnight, bad temper, rucksacks and suitcases full of dirty laundry, and endless cups of tea, all my love and thanks.

Finally, the views expressed on the following pages do not necessarily reflect those of the U.S. government, the Department of Defense, or the Department of the Army. I alone am responsible for the facts and opinions within the contents of this study.

Fort Bragg, North Carolina
May 1985

Chapter One

Conventional Defense

THE THEME OF THIS STUDY is that the conventional defense of Europe is achievable today, or in the near future, provided NATO is willing to think through the consequences; modify national and Alliance strategies; and accept a slightly higher, but not unacceptable, degree of near-term risk. This in no sense should give the impression that NATO is home free on conventional defense. On the contrary, given continuing Soviet modernization programs and the known deficiencies within the Alliance, especially in logistics, there is an urgent requirement to press ahead with what Henry Kissinger refers to as the "desperately needed NATO conventional buildup."[1] While some may question whether the need is desperate or just urgent, the current margin for successful conventional defense is too slim. Even under the best conditions, the Alliance's survival could depend on Soviet inefficiency and be threatened by relatively low-level tactical blunders of its own. Clearly, a buildup is required to provide some margin for error.

Moreover, neither will a strong conventional defense ever be a substitute for nuclear deterrence. It cannot. But, with the advent of essential nuclear parity at all levels, certain assumptions the West has made concerning the utility of nuclear weapons are now questionable. In 1946, writing about the effect of atomic weapons on military policy, Bernard Brodie said that "thus far the chief purpose of our military establishment has been to win wars. From now on its chief purpose must be to avert them. It can have almost no other useful purpose."[2] The extent to which his observation on nuclear arms has been stretched to include *all* military force is reflected today in the many references to "conventional deterrence." At any rate, Brodie's paradoxical view of the military's function—and strategy—is no longer as true as it seemed in 1946. The Soviets, who never have subscribed doctrinally to his view, understand that conventional superiority gives them real advantages, both politically and militarily. At the least, it opens opportunities for political intimidation. At worst, the Kremlin may someday believe that there is an "umbrella" of nuclear parity under which a conventional war may be fought to advantage. Soviet leaders may well imagine, in some crisis tomorrow or a decade from now, a conflict scenario in which the two sides withhold nuclear weapons use, fearing the consequences of uncontrollable escalation.[3] To borrow a phrase, a strong NATO conventional defense capability should be part of the "seamless garment" of deterrence, an equal part of a NATO defense policy that rests on a balance of nuclear and nonnuclear forces, as well as on political and economic strengths, that leads to a rational conclusion, and that denies any advantage to the Soviets which might tempt them in time of a crisis.

The recent public interest in nuclear deterrence is an opportunity for NATO to evolve a more balanced defense policy and strategy, one that includes adequate conventional defense as well as nuclear deterrence. There is also the possibility that, if no initiatives are taken, the public consensus for all defense will be weakened. This is not the time for long-term studies. The Alliance should seize the chance to capitalize on the emotions of the moment and install a strategy for Western defense that can survive the next one or two decades.

EVOLUTION: MASSIVE RETALIATION TO FLEXIBLE RESPONSE

For too long NATO has relied on nuclear weaponry for deterrence on the cheap. In 1951, Dean Acheson told Congress that "the best use we can make of our present advantage in retaliatory air power is to move ahead under this protective shield to build the balanced collective forces in Western Europe that will continue to deter aggression after our atomic advantage has diminished."[4] Despite his warnings, NATO has never developed a truly "balanced" force posture. The organization's current military policies have evolved through a period of initial confusion (post-World War II to about 1953), *massive retaliation* (1953–1967), and *flexible response* (1967 to the present). Two threads appear in Acheson's statement, however, that weave throughout the evolution of the West's military strategy.

The first is deterrence. From the beginning the whole purpose of NATO forces was to deter the Soviets from overt aggression against Western Europe. This postwar emphasis on deterrence through military power was ingrained in a generation that considered it had learned "the lessons of Munich" the hard way. In the minds of postwar statesmen, appeasement and weakness were the causes of the war, and they were determined never to repeat the error. The atomic bomb was also a major factor; its power and relative ease of employment were seen as such a revolutionary development that war might be impossible.

The second is Acheson's recognition that U.S. nuclear superiority would not last forever, and that NATO must eventually rely on "balanced collective forces" for its defense. In the immediate postwar period, however, the great task facing Western Europe was economic recovery, not remilitarization. To that end, the Marshall Plan was instituted in 1947, but robust prosperity was still a long way off in NATO's early years. Virtually the only members with strong economies and arsenals were the two Atlantic powers, Canada and the United States. As the strongest partner, the United States obviously had to take the lead in providing forces for Western defense in the postwar era.

Acheson's view prevailed throughout the Truman administration, with the adoption in 1950 of U.S. policy paper NSC-68, which proposed the creation of balanced military forces to deter Soviet aggression. The underlying assumption of NSC-68 was that, while nuclear superiority should be maintained, Communist aggression might be limited and executed in such a way that nuclear retaliation could be inappropriate. Implementation of NSC-68 was delayed by U.S. budget wrangles, but the North Korean invasion of the Republic of Korea that summer shocked both the United States and NATO into renewed urgency regarding the Alliance's conventional forces. In the immediate post-World War II period, there had been an effort to plan for a combined NATO conventional force to offset presumed Soviet conventional superiority. In the late 1940s various military regional planning groups had estimated that for the defense of Europe a total of 307 divisions would be required, or three times the Allied strength (less the Soviets), at the peak of the Second World War. Such a goal was plainly unaffordable, but it set a trend. Robert Osgood noted in 1968 that "ever since, the story of NATO, year by year, has been the slow whittling down of the soldiers' estimates of divisions needed for western defense from 307 to 96 and 70 to 60, and the subordination of their estimates to what the community can afford to pay."[5]

In 1950 the new Supreme Headquarters, Allied Powers Europe calculated the requirement at 96 divisions. But, at the Lisbon conference in 1952, the NATO governments postponed their goal and pledged instead to raise 50 active ground divisions by 1953; the schedule for future increases was left undecided.[6] (Today NATO counts about 30 divisions.)

The new U.S. administration that took office in 1953, however, believed that Western economic stability and progress could be endangered by defense budgets that were too large, and that Western prosperity was as important a long-term strategic weapon against the USSR as were large forces. American conventional forces, therefore, were cut back sharply, and in their place the Eisenhower administration chose to rely on the threat of massive nuclear retaliation to deter Communist aggression worldwide. The Strategic Air Command was equipped with combers of truly intercontinental reach, and medium bombers were deployed overseas in a ring around the Soviet Union. As a continuation of the emphasis on atomic warfare, tactical nuclear weapons were developed for use on the battlefield, and their deployment to Europe was begun.

So pervasive was the belief in the utility of nuclear fires that in 1954 the chairman of the U.S. Joint Chiefs of Staff, Admiral Arthur Radford, explained that atomic weapons had achieved virtually conventional status within the armed forces of the United States.[7] European governments and force planners followed the U.S. lead: the Lisbon goals were cut and then cut again. By 1957 NATO was planning to deploy only 30 active divisions in Europe. In 1957 it officially adopted massive retaliation as a strategy (MC document 14/2), thus calling for the early and extensive use of nuclear weapons in the event of an attack on NATO.

There were, however, critics of massive retaliation. Kissinger's *Nuclear Weapons and Foreign Policy* set the tone for the proponents of an alternate strategy. The new Democratic administration in 1961 brought into office policymakers who had serious doubts about 14/2, and under President John F. Kennedy and his secretary of defense, Robert S. McNamara, the United States began maneuvering for a change in U.S. and NATO strategy which would permit more Western flexibility. In particular, the United States began revitalizing its conventional forces and started edging away from massive retaliation.

NATO was skeptical when in 1962 McNamara proposed a new strategy of flexible response. To the Europeans it seemed like a rationale to weaken the link between the U.S. strategic nuclear deterrent and Europe. The French especially took exception and proceeded to develop their own independent nuclear force and to withdraw their forces from the military command, although France is still part of the Alliance. After much debate among the remaining members, a compromise was struck in 1967, with the official adoption of a flexible response strategy (or MC 14/3), which remains in effect today.

Flexible response, as delineated in 14/3, essentially says that the Alliance will seek to deter conflict, but, if deterrence fails, NATO will respond to aggression with forward defense at whatever level of hostilities the attack is initiated in an effort to make the enemy withdraw. To ensure a successful defense, however, NATO reserves the option to escalate the conflict, including the use of nuclear fires if necessary. Finally, 14/3 obligates the Alliance to recover whatever territory may have been lost during hostilities.

Flexible response and forward defense also have their critics, who generally fall into two groups. First are those who believe that 14/3 is an escalation ladder that NATO will inevitably climb if deterrence fails: "We fight with conventional weapons until we're losing, then we fight with tactical weapons until we're losing, then we blow up the world."[8] Second is the view that forward defense is operationally unworkable because it commits NATO forces too far forward to be soundly employed.

Both arguments can be rebutted. Escalation by NATO is only inevitable if deterrence fails and if aggression cannot be contained by conventional forces, which is the whole essence of this discussion. The alternative to forward defense is defense in depth, with West Germany providing the "depth." Aside from the Germans' understandable dismay at turning over their country to be a battleground, there is not much depth to give; it is about 130 miles from the intra-German border (IGB) to the French-Belgian border, or about twenty minutes' flying time in a relatively slow ground-attack aircraft. A shallow penetration of 100 kilometers on the North German Plain would sever Denmark and northern Germany from the central region. Fortunately, however, the area near the IGB favors an east-west defense. Forward defense also permits NATO to achieve a denser concentration of its mechanized and armored forces than if they were stationed further back where the defensive zone would be wider. Finally, a defense further back would leave NATO more vulnerable by reducing the protected rear area required to base aircraft, detect and destroy attacking enemy aircraft, and receive reinforcements.[9]

In retrospect, flexible response probably became inevitable once the Soviets deployed their own strategic missile force. When the American nuclear deterrent was delivered by short-range B-47s, the necessity for overseas basing made the European allies partners with the United States in nuclear deterrence. But, when the Soviets achieved a strategic nuclear capability and the U.S. retaliatory force was freed from dependence on European bases, the allies' role became passive, with the exception of the British and French who had their own forces. While the United States has never wavered in expressing its determination to support European security with the full weight of its nuclear arsenal, it should not have come as any surprise to Europe that the United States began looking for more nuclear maneuvering room as the Soviets developed a strategic delivery capability.

The end result of the evolution of nuclear weapons and strategy since World War II is the existence of roughly two schools of Western thought relative to nuclear deterrence. One favors improving and increasing NATO's conventional forces in order to gain more breathing room between the failure of deterrence and the last resort to nuclear weapons, which, even then, would be at the lowest level possible. This is generally the U.S. position. A second opinion believes that Western strategy should call for the early use of massive nuclear fire in the belief that such a strategy enhances deterrence by making the consequences of war so horrible that no aggressor would ever attempt an attack. This is generally the view held by Europeans who criticize the war-fighting position above because it makes a central front war believable.

NATO's dispositions today hint at a schizophrenic attitude toward nuclear weapons: the conventional forces stationed well forward in the Federal Republic of Germany are stronger than needed for a tripwire but not strong enough to fight a prolonged conventional defense. Furthermore, there seems to be thus far little exploration of the strategic implications of a conventional defense strategy in terms of the Alliance's traditional view of deterrence.

In the debate at this point there is a fortunate opportunity for consensus on the need for strong conventional defense, or rather for deemphasizing the reliance on nuclear weapons. From the Catholic bishops to the Harvard Nuclear Study Group, virtually every reputable pronouncement, study, and commission has recommended a buildup of conventional forces as a properly moral and pragmatic course for NATO to follow. The European Security Study has concluded that stronger conventional forces are needed to provide both deterrence and reassurance for NATO's populations. "The primary objective of the forces of the Alliance has been to present real and believable obstacles to any change in . . . Soviet caution, and to do it in ways that are also reassuring to the peoples of the Alliance."[10] The task now is to build on this consensus to install a long-range strategy before it evaporates or is preempted by more strident and less practical solutions.

THE CONTINENTALISTS AND MARITIMISTS

There is in the United States today a public discussion between strategists who center U.S. defense on Europe, with various versions of how the defense should be conducted, and strategists who emphasize sea power in a more unilateral approach to U.S. strategy. Ambassador Robert Komer, who argues that U.S. opposition to Soviet expansion should continue to be centered on the European continent, is a spokesman for the traditional Alliance strategy.[11] Komer and others, including the present Supreme Allied Commander Europe (SACEUR), General Bernard Rogers, say that conventional defense in Europe is possible if the allies are willing to pay the bill. Included in this view are many other articulate writers and strategists who, to enhance continental defense, would restructure forces, change forward defense policy, or press for greater burden-sharing among the allies. Komer has remarked that "any NATO conventional option must be seen from the outset as financially achievable in order to generate the . . . necessary resources to carry it out." He suggests five areas in which the present NATO force structure should be improved: increasing war reserve stocks, providing additional reserve formations, building up infrastructure such as airfields and aircraft shelters, improving NATO's air defense capability, and placing greater stress on low-cost barrier options.[12]

General Rogers believes that NATO conventional inferiority in Europe leaves the nuclear threshold at a disturbingly low level. As a solution he proposes an upgrading of existing forces, modernization, and technological means to delay, disrupt, and destroy enemy forces deep behind the lines of contact. His formula for achieving such capabilities is increased defense spending by NATO members. "The achievement of an adequate conventional deterrent by the end of the decade requires annual real increases in defense spending somewhat higher than the three per cent agreed to by NATO nations."[13]

Politically, the Komer and Rogers views are acceptable to NATO because they support the status quo and turn the strategic debate into a budgetary one, and NATO's members have thick hides and great expertise in dealing with strategy as a function of budgets. The idea of conventional NATO offensive strategies as a way to enforce conventional deterrence has recently emerged. The most articulate spokesman for this view thus far is Professor Samuel Huntington, who argues that "there is no reason why a defensive alliance cannot have an offensive strategy." Huntington's major point is that NATO's conventional strategy should have an offensive component, which he presents as a plan to launch, immediately upon the outbreak of war, a retaliatory offensive into Eastern Europe. With such a strategy, he believes, the West would be better able to diversify its deterrent policies and achieve a greater degree of confidence in overall deterrence. "NATO strategy has given the Soviet offensive a free ride," he writes; "if, however, the Soviets had to consider the possibility of a prompt NATO conventional offensive, they would either have to reallocate forces from offensive to defensive missions or to devote still more scarce resources to military purposes to meet this need."[14]

There are objections to this view. Huntington's proposal amounts to "Sovietizing" NATO strategy and violates what is understood as the fundamental spirit of the NATO Alliance. Richard Sinnrich has noted that "any attempt by the United States to press an offensive conventional strategy on NATO is likely to confirm already widespread European doubts about America's strategic prudence; and, in the process, still further diminish the perception of common security interests essential to continued alliance cohesion."[15] Although Huntington tends to play down the need for additional forces, they would unquestionably be required to mount and support an early offensive into Eastern Europe. It is not clear whether adopting such a strategy would enhance conventional defense; it is clear that Sovietizing NATO's conventional defense is politically unacceptable as well as militarily infeasible at present.

The maritime strategists tend to focus on U.S. interests in the Third World and the Pacific. They nod toward Europe but believe that the struggle between democracy and totalitarianism is ultimately going to be decided outside NATO. By unduly concentrating resources on Europe, they say, the United States restricts its ability to protect its out-of-area interests. If an unlikely war did break out in Europe, U.S. naval power would be an appropriate and effective contribution to NATO defense; it would strike at the Soviet Union directly and convoy reinforcements rapidly to the Continent. Admiral (ret.) Stansfield Turner and Captain George Thibault contend that "the United States has consistently failed to meet its military commitments in other parts of the world."[16] An adjunct of this argument, also heard among the continentalists, is that Europeans must take up a greater share of the defense load in Europe. The divergence between sea power-land power advocates occurs when the maritime strategists conclude that, if Europe does not pay its bills, the United States would be justified in withdrawing some land forces, presumably then funding more sea power. Jeffrey Record, a maritime spokesman, takes this position.[17]

To the sea power advocates, Komer replies, correctly, that a U.S. move toward a maritime strategy, as outlined, would be destructive of American interests in NATO. "Our already restive allies would correctly perceive such a US strategy as at best a form of unilateral US global interventionism and at worst a form of neoisolationism. Pressures for accommodation with the Soviet Union would be powerfully enhanced."[18] But the sea power advocates also seem justified in their misgivings about the continued business-as-usual strategy in Europe which involves the United States in an open-ended commitment without definable military objectives, or even a definition of military success if deterrence fails.

On closer examination much of the land power-sea power debate has echoes of frustration over Brodie's paradox and the unwinnability of war in Europe: if conventional forces cannot win there, then the money might be better spent elsewhere. This kind of reaction seems to be a hangover from decades of reliance on nuclear deterrence, or from a conceptual vacuum concerning any conventional defense options other than a futile defense leading to negotiation or nuclear war. The strategy debate rarely extends beyond D-day force ratios, or, at most, the first days of combat. In exculpation of the experts, it is very difficult to model prolonged combat rigorously. Assumptions multiply in almost geometric progression. How did the war start? Did the Dutch reserves reach their positions? Did the French come in? Gaming all the various forces—sea, land, and air—is complex and costly in terms of expert manpower. Logistics studies are especially demanding. Basic assumptions are so loaded with service budgetary implications that getting military professionals into a truly neutral game is difficult.[19] But the reward is a glimpse of possibilities for conventional defense strategy. One of those glimpses reveals a conjunction of maritime and continental strategies, as will be discussed, which leads one to suspect that the horizons of the debate are too limited.[20]

The key to enlarging the strategic horizon is found at two levels. The first is to evolve a short-range practical concept of how NATO can be defended with existing forces, or forces that already have been budgeted and also have utility elsewhere. Beyond that a resolution of NATO's open-ended strategic dilemma must be found in a way that acknowledges nuclear weapons and protects the politically sensitive defensive nature of the Alliance. The catchphrase "restore the territory of the Alliance" provides a goal but not a military objective or concept. This study offers a partial answer; it deals with an initial defense and the capability to execute continued operations beyond the first defensive phase.

MYTHS

Some myths should be laid to rest. First, it is not entirely clear that the West need spend inordinately large amounts on increasing the numbers of available conventional forces, or reequipping standing units. James Hollingsworth has written:

> With respect to the costs of the conventional umbrella, great concern has been expressed about the cost of sophisticated technology. . . . Many estimates indicate that the development, procurement, operational and maintenance costs for this capability over 10 years is about $10 billion to $15 billion . . . if we pursue this with NATO, the US costs would be much less, perhaps no more than half. This is equivalent to about 350 F-15 aircraft, or about 2,500 M-1 tanks, or about 10 DDG-51s, or the manpower costs for one and one-half US divisions for 10 years.[21]

Other authorities have estimated that a more secure NATO conventional defense capability can be had if the European member nations add about 1 percent to the current levels of expenditure.[22] General Rogers has been attempting for several years to convince these nations to increase their defense spending for conventional weapons. The results, unfortunately, have been mixed for reasons having as much to do with economics as political will. It should be remembered too that European NATO defense spending, on the whole, increased by about 2 percent per year in the 1970s, while U.S. spending in real terms was declining. Additionally, economic recovery in Europe in 1984 lagged behind that of the United States. Even with current levels of spending, however, the larger European allies—Britain, France, and West Germany—field large well-equipped forces, with West Germany and France also providing great numbers of territorial or homeguard type formations.

Second, it should never be assumed that increased defense expenditures for conventional forces are part of a strategy to trap the Soviets in an exhausting arms race. Nothing could be more futile or less productive. Although the Soviets are having serious economic problems, they have shown no inclination to back away from increased defense spending. Their closed economy gives them far more flexibility to match the West in terms of capital accumulation, standardization, and captive markets. The Politburo has the authority to make budget decisions without regard to consumer pressure, although it has not been conclusively proven that the Soviets budget their defense forces in response to what they see as the Western threat. In fact, Soviet procurement seems to have proceeded with some indifference as to what the United States or NATO does. Harold Brown's comment that, when we build, they build; when we stop, they build, emphasizes the point that Soviet military spending has been regular, growing, and independent of any arms race against the West.

Other major objections to preparing a conventional defense of Europe tend to center around the near-term conventional military imbalance in Europe and NATO's vulnerability to surprise attack. Lenin is reported to have said that "quantity has a quality all its own,"[23] and Soviet military planners seem to have taken his remark to heart. The NATO-Warsaw Pact military balance is distinctly unfavorable to the West when total numbers of tanks, troops, and combat aircraft are presented. NATO claims, for example, that the Warsaw Pact disposes of about 4 million men under arms versus its 2.6 million, 42,500 main battle tanks versus 13,000, and 24,300 antitank missile launchers compared to 8,100.[24]

Numbers do count, both at the point of battle and as replacements for combat attrition. Moreover, the importance of standing forces versus long-term military industrial potential has grown sharply since World War II. The complexity of modern weapons systems argues powerfully that under present conditions, without considerable and unlikely attention to mobilization planning, industrial base surges will not be able to offset inadequate numbers in the early stages of future conflict. F-16 fighters cannot be mass-produced the way P-40s were in 1942.

Numbers, however, also can mislead. Any strategist who begins to dip into figures for comparison immediately becomes mired down in what the military calls "bean counting," in which there are many ways to count forces on either side. For example, NATO's count given above does not include France, which is still a member and still stations forces forward on German soil, nor do they account for European forces not assigned to NATO. When French manpower alone is added, as it almost surely would be, the balance becomes over 3 million men versus 4 million and over 15,000 tanks compared to 42,500. The bulk of the West German Territorial Army, a force of about 38,000, and reserve personnel, which in the Federal Republic alone number 500,000, is likewise not counted. Strictly speaking, NATO is correct not to count forces not actually assigned. Practically, however, they should be considered. When they are, the overall numbers still picture an imbalance, but certainly not a hopeless one.

When geography and Soviet dispositions are taken into account, it can be seen that the Soviets man their eastern and southern borders with 80 of their 191 combat divisions, or 41 percent of their ground forces. The Soviet units in the east and south can be made available to the central front but only with difficulty, only after the initial phase of the war, and only with the Soviets taking, as they would see it, grave risks. Most likely they would pass over the nuclear threshold before moving the substantial mass of their far eastern ground forces away from the Chinese border.

In terms of manpower, John Collins has calculated that in 1980 the central European balance was just less than 1 million NATO personnel to 1,384,000 Warsaw Pact, 23 to 58 available divisions, and nearly 9,000 tanks to 25,000.[25] Robert Fischer bases his study on fighting power, calculating that NATO has 414,000 men in its combat divisions, while the Pact has 564,000.[26] Clearly, relying just on numbers can be tricky.

What really counts in a conventional defense is the force ratio at the point of contact over time. For the Soviets the essential problem would be to mass sufficient forces to achieve a breakthrough. For this reason they emphasize the virtues of overwhelming force at critical points. The U.S. Army believes that it takes a ratio of about six attackers to one defender to achieve a decisive breakthrough.[27] Failing this, the attacker can attempt to make up the force shortfall with firepower, surprise, or skill.

In the massing of forces, however, the Soviets face a number of obstacles, among which are geography, the loss of surprise, exposure to prolonged attack by Western air power, and congestion. Given reasonable warning, NATO could shift forces to threatened sectors to prevent the kind of breakthrough mass that could lead to Soviet success. NATO and the individual Alliance members are investing heavily in the kinds of surveillance systems that would enable the Alliance to look deeply into the enemy rear to detect these moves. The coordination of deep air strikes against Warsaw Pact armies, as they mass and move toward an attack, has been the subject of intense NATO doctrinal study for the past several years.

It is NATO's lack of sufficient reserves to reinforce critical points, or to take advantage of Pact weaknesses elsewhere, that is the Alliance's greatest conventional fault today. Given NATO's total forces, however, there should be enough troops and time, although just barely, to build such reserves provided the Alliance moves decisively in the early stages of a Warsaw Pact attack. Such a strategy could be defeated by a surprise Soviet assault that takes NATO totally unaware; this is possible but unlikely. The Alliance or its members also could fail to mobilize in the face of a warning, but this too is not probable.

The Soviet Union today has the capability to launch a unilateral, limited surprise attack against NATO with very little warning. The major objection to its doing so is political; under present conditions the Soviet leadership does not want war in the central region any more than the West does. The fact that they may not want it for different reasons is immaterial. A "bolt from the blue" supposes that the Kremlin can make a cold-blooded decision to attack without strategic warning, without allies, and with a hope of some kind of political gain.

Militarily, the invading forces could not be reinforced easily since mobilization would have been sacrificed for strategic surprise and other Pact forces would not be available. The unreinforced Soviet forces entering West Germany would probably enjoy initial success and then would be chopped up in fairly short order by an aroused NATO. For these reasons, which will be discussed in more detail elsewhere, surprise attack is a low-priority problem.

MOBILIZATION

If a no-notice surprise attack by the Soviet Union is the most likely threat, then standing forces, not NATO mobilization, are the main issue. If, on the other hand, it is likely that there will be a period of tension, followed by an unmistakable Pact mobilization of uncertain size, then NATO mobilization is the issue. In all probability, time will be available for some Western mobilization, or, if NATO cannot achieve consensus, for independent action among its members.

The prospect of the military forces of NATO complacently watching a Soviet and Warsaw Pact mobilization is unlikely. It clearly would be in the common interest if, in the face of mobilization by the other side, NATO could take the lead in coordinating Western mobilization, which it probably would. The often repeated fear, however, that Alliance mobilization could be held up by one or two foot-dragging votes most likely would not happen. Individual countries within the Alliance can, and probably would, begin their own mobilizations with or without NATO sanction if the threat was serious enough. West Germany and the United States, in particular, can mobilize bilaterally without having to wait. The lights might not be burning all night in Brussels, but they would be in Stuttgart and Fulda. This is not meant to advocate unilateral mobilization but to remove the issue of whether or not NATO or its members will mobilize. Whether mobilization occurs as an Alliance, or as a result of the larger states, which generally have access to the most reliable technical intelligence, acting independently and dragging NATO behind them is moot for the purpose of this discussion. The important point is how the process may be used both as a deterrence signal and to posture forces more effectively.

One of the implications of moving toward a conventional defense strategy in Europe is that mobilization becomes a deterrent tool to a far greater degree than it is today. Mobilization deterrence may well take its place next to nuclear deterrence as a strategy designed to avert war by signaling NATO's determination, to prevent Warsaw Pact surprise, and to get ahead of the "mobilization curve" in a way that calculably prevents a favorable correlation of forces in the Soviet viewpoint.

Mobilization deterrence worked poorly in 1914. In that year it was not linked to deterrence, nor was it subject to overhead observation, television broadcasting, or the kind of close control that could be exercised today if the West so chose. Every politician's nightmare is, or should be, of Germany's General Helmuth von Moltke's argument to Kaiser Wilhelm on the night of 1 August 1914: "Those arrangements took a whole year of intricate labor to complete . . . and once settled, it cannot be altered."[28] But mobilization or reinforcement of NATO is essential in crisis; the question is how to make it usable.

To become a deterrent tool, NATO mobilization needs to be improved and exercised, particularly in the aspects of control by policymakers and the signals inherent in various kinds of mobilization and reinforcement. The United States is investing heavily in improved reinforcement capability, considering the annual *Reforger* exercises, the attention being paid to prestocking and strategic mobility, and efforts under way to improve the U.S. planning systems. What is needed now is an understanding of the role all these factors could play in pre-D-day deterrence, Alliance reassurance, and posturing for a war both sides probably would be trying to avoid. Mobilization is conceptually difficult to plan and expensive to practice; nevertheless, if the Alliance is to address conventional defense seriously, mobilization plays a vital role.

THE DISTANT VIEW

In addition to the short-term political and military benefits of moving toward an enhanced NATO conventional defense, there is likely to be a more subtle benefit to both the United States, NATO, and the West in general over the long term. War in Europe is the most serious, but least likely, contingency the West must face in the coming decades. Of more immediate importance is the way the West will deal with the political and economic impact of the developing nations as they emerge on the world scene. In this, the maritimists are correct.

Whether NATO ever addresses Third World concerns as an alliance, or the member nations unilaterally come to their own approaches, making NATO less dependent on the U.S. nuclear deterrent will probably encourage the European members to resume broader roles, implicit in which is the use of military power, that they have lately played in securing their own interests. The best-case proof of this is France which, when it left the military structure, took back its traditional independence. In the process it has reestablished itself as an important and independent force in the Third World. France's deployment of forces, most recently to Chad, and its cooperation in the Beirut peace-keeping force in 1983, are two examples. Britain continues to be influential in many Third World countries, especially in the Middle East and the Persian Gulf area. Strong economic growth, which in modern terms means international trade, and confidence in a strong conventional defense are keys to the eventual possibility of weaning NATO away from relying solely on U.S. nuclear weapons without destroying confidence in American dedication to the Alliance. The interests of the United States are better served in a world of strong democracies than weaker ones, even when they compete and disagree.

Stronger and more self-reliant NATO countries are vital to the West's long-term relations with struggling underdeveloped nations, many of which have historic European associations. The United States is not omnipotent; other free countries with different historical backgrounds and geographical associations may be more easily approached by Third World states. While only the United States is uniquely prepared to play the major role of maintaining the global balance with the Soviet Union, European countries, either as an entity or individually, can and should play a greater part in the critical task of easing the developing nations into the economic, social, and political mainstream. Thus, by steering NATO away from exclusive dependence on nuclear weapons, the members of the Alliance should be able to turn their attention in security matters toward a more multidimensional view of the world. In the long run this may be what counts most of all.

Notes

[1] Henry A. Kissinger, "A Plan to Reshape NATO," *Time* 123, no. 10 (5 March 1984): 21.

[2] Bernard Brodie, *The Absolute Weapon: Atomic Power and World Order* (New York: Harcourt, Brace, 1946), p. 76. Brodie's observation must be read in the context of the times when the United States enjoyed absolute nuclear superiority. Russell F. Weigley, in *The American Way of War* (Bloomington: Indiana University Press, 1973), does an excellent job of highlighting the strategic and budgetary disputes within the U.S. government in the late 1940s and early 1950s when Brodie's view of deterrence had its greatest impact.

[3] Bernard W. Rogers, "Raising the Nuclear Threshold," *Defense '84*, June 1984, p. 6.

[4] Quoted in Robert E. Osgood, "Rearmament and Relaxation," in Lawrence S. Kaplan, ed., *NATO and the Policy of Containment* (Lexington, MA: D. C. Heath, 1968), p. 56.

[5] Ibid., p. 63.

[6] Ibid.

[7] Arthur W. Radford, "Strong U.S. Defense for the Long Pull," *U.S. News and World Report* (5 March 1954): 50.

[8] Morton S. Halpern, in Hearings Before the Subcommittee on U.S. Security Agreements and Commitments Abroad and the Subcommittee on Arms Control, International Law and Organization of the Committee on Foreign Relations, quoted in "Military Issues Research Memorandum," *NATO Defense Posture in an Environment of Strategic Parity and Precision Weaponry* (Carlisle Barracks, PA: U.S. Army War College Strategic Studies Institute, 1978), p. 11. Halpern's quote is widely found in discussions of defense policy; the author heard it misquoted by an antinuclear activist in Canada.

[9] Phillip A. Karber, "In Defense of Forward Defense," *Armed Forces Journal* 121, no. 10 (May 1984): 27–50. Excellent article and one that discusses in detail why forward defense is both necessary and workable, with much data not usually found elsewhere.

[10] European Security Study (EES), *Strengthening Conventional Deterrence in Europe* (New York: St. Martin's Press, 1983), p. 7. The Steering Committee's articulation of the need for deterrence and reassurance is a major point that needs to be considered in all Alliance defense debate. An excellent, although less enthusiastic, commentary on the consensus for conventional defense is Catherine Kelleher, "Nuclear-Conventional Tradeoffs: The Debate in Europe," in Keith A. Dunn and William O. Staudenmaier, eds., *Military Strategy in Transition: Defense and Deterrence in the 1980s* (Carlisle Barracks, PA: U.S. Army War College, 1984), pp. 84–96.

[11] Robert W. Komer, "Maritime Strategy Versus Coalition Defense," *Foreign Affairs* 60, no. 5 (Summer 1982): 1124–44.

[12] Robert W. Komer, "Costs and Benefits of a Low-Cost Conventional Component," *Armed Forces Journal* 121, no. 10 (May 1984): 112–16.

[13] Rogers, "Raising the Nuclear Threshold," pp. 2–7.

[14] Samuel Huntington, "Conventional Deterrence and Conventional Retaliation in Europe," in Dunn and Staudenmaier, *Military Strategy in Transition* (Boulder, CO: Westview Press, 1984), p. 27.

[15] Richard W. Sinnrich, "Strategic Implications of Doctrinal Change: A Case Analysis," ibid., p. 56.

[16] Stansfield Turner and George Thibault, "Preparing for the Unexpected: The Need for a New Military Strategy," *Foreign Affairs* 61, no. 1 (Fall 1982): 124.

[17] Jeffrey Record, "Is Europe Defensible?" *Baltimore Sun*, 19 April 1984.

[18] Komer, "Maritime Strategy," p. 1134.

[19] At least two other strategists apparently feel this way. See Keith A. Dunn and William O. Staudenmaier, "Strategy for Survival," *Foreign Policy*, no. 52 (Fall 1983): 22–41.

[20] A result of the frustration with a no-win strategic view has been to turn the energies of the services toward budget battles. Colonel Staudenmaier writes that "it is not to disparage the integrity of the continental or maritime schools to suggest that thus far the . . . debate has all the overtones of a service budget debate with enough strategic fluff to give it respectability." See Staudenmaier, "One if by Land, Two if by Sea: The Continental-Maritime Debate in Perspective," *Army* 33, no. 1 (January 1983): 37.

[21] James F. Hollingsworth, "Understanding the Conventional Umbrella," *Armed Forces Journal* 121, no. 7 (February 1984): 46.

[22] See International Institute for Strategic Studies, *The Military Balance, 1983–1984* (London: IISS, 1983), p. 25.

[23] Quoted in John M. Collins, *U.S.-Soviet Military Balance, 1960–1980* (Washington, DC: McGraw-Hill, 1980), p. 425.

[24] North Atlantic Treaty Organization, *NATO and the Warsaw Pact: Force Comparisons* (undated fact sheet), pp. 9, 11.

[25] Collins, *Military Balance*, p. 542.

[26] Robert Lucas Fischer, "Defending the Central Front," quoted in John J. Mearsheimer, "Why the Soviets Can't Win Quickly in Central Europe," *International Security* 7, no. 1 (Summer 1982): 7.

[27] U.S. Army, *FM 100-5, Operations* (Washington, DC: Government Printing Office, 1976), p. 3–4 [hereafter cited as *Operations* (1976)]. Although this manual has been superseded by a 1982 edition, the factual data remain valid.

[28] Quoted in Barbara Tuchman, *The Guns of August* (New York: Macmillan, 1962), pp. 99–100.

Chapter Two

NATO's Central Front

THE THEATER

THE FRONT LINE in the East-West confrontation is the IGB, running from Lübeck on the Baltic for 750 kilometers past Wolfsburg, Göttingen, Coburg, and Bayreuth where East Germany stops and the border becomes West Germany-Czechoslovakia, then extending south to Passau where neutral Austria comes in on the shoulders of the rugged Alps. With its flanks thus anchored on the sea to the north and the mountains on the south, the IGB divides more than Germany and Europe. It is the limit of Communist authority toward the West, the highwater mark of the Red Army of World War II and its line of departure for any prospective further campaigning.

The most significant military feature of European geography is the broad northern plain that begins deep in the Soviet Union and runs along the littoral of first the Baltic and then the North Sea, bending downward as the coast curves and finally ending on the Bay of Biscay at the neck of the Iberian peninsula. Industry, population centers, and seaports have grown up along this avenue of broad fields and numerous north-flowing rivers, especially west of the Danish peninsula where access to the North Sea and the English Channel has encouraged international commerce since early history. East of Denmark the East German-Polish littoral is not so developed except on the very edge of the sea. In the west, inland cities like Hamburg, Bremen, Amsterdam, Antwerp, and Brussels lie close to the coast. With the exception perhaps of a few smaller cities, such as Lübeck and Gdansk, there is no comparable buildup eastward.

Dotted by nature with thousands of small lakes from the east to the Elbe and by man with crops and villages, the North

German Plain forms a natural corridor for east-west movement, a fact that has not escaped potential invaders. In modern times the invasion plans of two German reichs have rested on the sweep of great armies along this plain through the Low Countries, whose governments have vainly attempted to remain neutral despite the geography that makes them the doorway to Paris. Like the Shenandoah Valley of the American Civil War, the route of the plain favors an attack in only one direction. Traveled westward, it leads directly to the heart of Western Europe, placing an invading army across the enemy's industrial heartland and near every major West European capital save Bonn. Traveled eastward, an army skirts Berlin, a major transportation hub for East Germany, and then launches into the flat, lake-spotted emptiness of East Prussia and northern Poland.

To the south, Europe's topography begins to jumble with rolling and broken foothills and valleys, increasing in number and relief as they move toward the Alps. Again, looking at the ground from a military perspective, two approaches less promising than the plain breach the mountain barrier along the East German and Czech borders (see Map 1). The first of these, called the Fulda Gap, begins in East Germany in the vicinity of Weimar and cuts southwestward across the border before ending in the densely built-up region around Frankfurt. The second is the Hof Corridor, which drives from Leipzig almost directly south through Hof and Bayreuth toward Nuremberg. To an attacker from the east, both routes have the strategic disadvantage of pointing deeper into the center of the European mass, as opposed to the North German Plain route that strikes more directly at industrial areas and national capitals near the coast. Traveling the other way, however, the Fulda and Hof avenues lead into the heart of East Germany and into the East European populations. In the south the Shenandoah Valley example is reversed.

Europe's political divisions have played an important role in determining conventional defense strategies. The two most important factors have been the configuration of the Federal Republic and the withdrawal of French forces from NATO in 1967, which also resulted in the eviction of U.S. forces from France. For the West Germans, whose country would provide the initial battleground for a European war between NATO

Map 1. Three Pact Avenues of Attack

Source: Adapted from Richard D. Lawrence and Jeffrey Record, *U.S. Force Structure in NATO: An Alternative* (Washington, DC: Brookings Institution, 1974), p. 31. Reprinted by permission of the Brookings Institution.

and the Warsaw Pact, the narrowness of their country precludes any kind of defense predicated on trading space for time; they have no space to give. At West Germany's narrow waist the entire country is only about 220 kilometers wide, or about the distance between Washington, DC, and Philadelphia.[1] The 1979 German White Paper on Defense puts it succinctly:

> For the Federal Republic of Germany, there can be no alternative to forward defence: in view of her geostrategic situation, her population density near the border to the

> Warsaw Pact, and the structure of her economy, any conceptual model of defence involving the surrender of territory is unacceptable. Thirty per cent of the population live in a 100 kilometre-wide zone this side of the intra-German border, and twenty-five per cent of our industrial capacity is located in that zone. These geographic circumstances rule out any defensive operations conducted flexibly in the depth of the area and accepting the loss of territory. Such a concept of operations would not be in accordance with the mission to preserve the integrity of our territory.[2]

The vulnerability of the West German heartland to Pact armored columns, and an understandable desire to avoid having that country devastated by conventional war, also lead the Federal Republic to rely on the American nuclear shield to a greater degree than any other NATO country. When forward defending units are seen as tripwire forces, then nuclear and conventional doctrines come together, which sums up the West German position.

The withdrawal of France from active participation in NATO exacerbated the difficulty of maintaining a forward defense posture. First, NATO lost maneuvering room for positioning and basing forces as well as for planning military operations. Even if the Federal Republic had been willing to plan a defense in depth, the loss of French soil made such a concept difficult. In the event of war, all NATO European soil could be reasonably expected to be open for maneuver, but, to the extent that peacetime planning and training influences strategy and forces in war, the loss of France has put conceptual blinders on European strategy and perhaps contributed to the perception of forward defense as an all-or-nothing tripwire for nuclear weapons use.

Second, and of more significance, NATO logistic lines of communication through France were lost. Without France, allied supply lines were forced to move to German and Dutch ports closer to the IGB and well within range of Pact surface-to-surface missiles and air strikes. At present, the main land lines of communication (LOC) start at Bremerhaven, Rotterdam, and Antwerp and then run south behind and parallel to the prospective front where they could be quickly overtaken. NATO's airfields also have been forced to deploy forward, making them vulnerable to quick strikes. While France would probably reenter the Alliance in an emergency, the constitution of logistic facilities under emergency conditions, complicated by road nets that tend to run north-south instead of east-west, would be a difficult undertaking.

THE FORCES

Historical experience and asymmetries in strategic and operational doctrine have led to differences in the military organizations of the United States, Western Europe, and the Soviet bloc. Although European and American reserve philosophies both draw from the Napoleonic *levée en masse*, in Europe and the Soviet Union reserve forces have been historically and doctrinally closer to the mainstream of traditional military strategy and policy. From the Napoleonic Wars until the present day, in fact, the great powers of Europe, with the possible exception of Great Britain, based their national military strategies on the capabilities of their mobilized reserves rather than on the strengths of their regular formations alone. The Prussians came as close to perfecting reserve mobilization as anyone has ever done: the German right wing that swept through Belgium in August 1914 was composed largely of reserve formations, and their excellence surprised the French who had considered that reservists would be less effective than regulars. In Europe today armies on each side of the Iron Curtain count on reservists; for example, West Germany's Territorial Army of mixed regulars and reservists stands behind the regular Field Army, and behind both is a pool of about 2 million former servicemen with reserve obligations. The Red Army, to a large extent, is a reservist's army; well over one-half of its divisions are at reduced manning, and reserve obligations for males in the USSR extend until age fifty.[3] In states where conscription is the rule, the reserve formations are composed mostly of soldiers who have served in the active forces but who have a continuing reserve obligation.

The United States also has a strong reserve tradition, dating from the militias of the eighteenth century and updated by Napoleonic concepts imported in the early nineteenth. The U.S. case, however, stresses a decentralized system controlled more by the states than by the federal government. In the

American experience, reserve mobilization has tended to be more leisurely than the European model and is normally followed by a prolonged training period. Reserve units were not even called in during the Vietnam War except for a few specialized formations.

In the post-World War II debate over European defense policy, the nature of massive retaliation tended to play down the importance of reserve formations in the United States. If the forces in Europe were to be tripwires for nuclear retaliation, not only would there be insufficient time for U.S. reserves to mobilize and deploy, but also they would not be necessary. Flexible response provided a strategic rationale for reserve mobilization as part of a larger conventional defense, but budgetary pressures and European fears of a prolonged war made a genuine upgrading of reserve mobilization capabilities a low-priority item in defense budgets. If, however, NATO moves toward reliance on mobilization and conventional defense to deter aggression, U.S. reserve forces will play a center stage role.[4]

Force balances alone tend to be an unsatisfactory method of accounting for NATO and Warsaw Pact capabilities. They cannot be dispensed with entirely, but their true significance only comes to light—imperfect light at that—when other factors, such as political circumstances, military doctrines, and geography, are considered. What follows is an attempt to recapitulate forces relevant to conventional defense and to relate them to the doctrinal, topographical, and political environment in which war in Europe might be conducted.

THE UNITED STATES

The United States has not had to consider seriously a land threat to its territory since the War of 1812. Historically, the nation has relied on a strong navy and a small peacetime standing army, backed by a large reserve, or militia. Its experience in this century has been with wars fought abroad by armies raised in the security of the United States and convoyed overseas by a powerful navy. In time of crisis the regular army raised, trained, and directed the employment of the citizen army which fought the big battles. Although peacetime service in the active forces was not traditional, there was a strong tradition of part-time soldiering in the local militia, which became in the twentieth century the National Guard or reserve units of the various services. This practice was overturned in 1948 when apprehension over postwar Soviet intentions led to the first U.S. peacetime draft, which continued until it was discredited by the Vietnam War and ended in 1974. The fact that the United States maintained its overseas commitments in spite of its maritime traditions and isolationist tendency partly explains why its force structure, which is sensitive to legislative budget pressures, tends to get out of synchronization with strategy in the postwar era.

Generally the composition of U.S. forces has varied throughout the post-World War II years as American security policies have changed. In contrast to the Europeans, who have focused consistently on the security of Western Europe, the United States has security interests around the world. A collection of treaties and agreements obligates the United States to help defend countries in Latin America, Japan, Korea, and other Asian states along the eastern Soviet rim as well as Western Europe. In addition, America has assumed defense obligations without formal treaties to many others such as Israel and the pro-Western Arab states in the Persian Gulf region. The U.S. view of its responsibilities, however, is ranked in order of priority, and none is as compelling as those associated with NATO.[5]

The end of the draft and cuts in service manpower and funding during the post-Vietnam period caught the U.S. armed forces, and the army in particular, between unchanged demands, reduced assets, and an increased Soviet threat. In fact, security requirements actually grew in the 1970s during a time when army divisional strength sagged from 16 active duty divisions to 13 and then gradually built back up to 16.[6] (A recent initiative by the army plans to add 2 light divisions to the force structure by the end of the decade, bringing the total of active divisions up to 18.) Active manpower dropped from 1,314,000 to 758,000. The price of stretching U.S. ground manpower so thin was to cut back on combat support units and to maintain some division organizations at below strength status. In some cases, divisions were cut to two-thirds their normal combat organization, with wartime augmentation planned from the National Guard.

As far as land combat was concerned, the drop in manpower was to be offset by increased firepower and mobility derived from the American lead in technology over the Soviet Union and its allies. Dependence on high-technology weaponry was explicit in the assumptions that validated the American move to an all-volunteer force, although there is some doubt that combat formations actually decreased in size; whole support units, however, were transferred from active to reserve status.[7] During the same period, the destructive capability of modern weaponry, particularly antitank weapons, convinced U.S. defense planners that any conflict involving U.S.- and Soviet-style armies would be short and extremely violent. This belief was reinforced by studies of the 1973 Arab-Israeli War, in which both sides experienced high rates of attrition and munition consumption. The introduction to the 1976 edition of the U.S. Army's standard manual on military operations asserted that

> Because the lethality of modern weapons continues to increase sharply, we can expect very high losses to occur in very short periods of time. Entire forces could be destroyed quickly if they are improperly employed.
> Therefore the first battle of our next war could well be its last battle: belligerents could be quickly exhausted and international pressures to stop fighting could bring about an early cessation of hostilities. The United States could find itself in a short, intense war—the outcome of which may be dictated by the results of initial combat. . . . Today the US Army must, above all else, *prepare to win the first battle of the next war.* Once the war is upon us, we shall aim at emerging triumphant from the second, third and final battles as well.[8]

Because of the U.S. emphasis on the first battle and the need "to fight outnumbered and win" in any conflict, especially in Europe, the structure of U.S. Army divisions from the early 1970s onward was clearly toward heavy mechanized or armored divisions tailored to fight Soviet armor.[9] The emphasis on the short war scenario and winning the first battle was supported therefore by the two assumptions that a small U.S. volunteer force would have to depend on sophisticated weaponry to offset numerical inferiority, and that any future battles would be so violent that their intensity would quickly exhaust both combatants. In a European scenario in particular, there was an expectation that the war would probably be settled before mobilization would have any effect. This view was generally accepted because it reflected combat results from the Mideast, defined "success" within the bounds of U.S. capabilities, and fitted in with the European preferred forward defense concept of a short, violent conflict along the IGB, followed by either an unlikely "conflict termination," or the more likely use of nuclear weapons before central Europe became a battleground for a protracted conventional war. For a military strategist trying to visualize continued conventional operations, there was a kind of operational blank wall beyond the first battle.

The emphasis on quick decision in Europe led, in times of fiscal restraint, to a decline in the U.S. ability to mobilize and deploy forces. Unglamorous airlift, sea transports, and tankers required to move and sustain overseas forces were generally low-priority items in service budgets. The Merchant Marine, which would provide most of the break-bulk shipping for the vast tonnages of supplies required in the event of a European war, dropped precipitately. Charter cargo ships, the backbone of the Vietnam support fleet, decreased from 123 in 1970 to 22 in 1979, while charter tankers dropped from 36 to 8 during the same period. Amphibious shipping (vessels designed to unload fighting units directly onto contested beaches) declined as well. The U.S. Navy's destroyer strength, which would provide essential convoy escort and antisubmarine warfare (ASW), dropped from 159 active ships in 1970 to 75 in 1979; frigates, which also provide ASW, increased but just by 20 vessels.[10] Only military airlift showed an increase, but the intensive planning, begun as part of the formation of the Rapid Deployment Force in 1980, showed existing and proposed airlift to be insufficient and unsuited to haul the kinds of bulk required to reinforce ground forces substantially with heavy tanks and other modern equipment.[11]

Acceptance of the short war overlooked the fact that, if the army's doctrine had changed, American strategy had not; the United States still planned to reinforce Europe with large numbers of divisions and manpower fillers from the continental United States. As the decade went by a three-way mismatch developed among the strategy that called for masses of conventional forces, the doctrine that required high-technology, hard-hitting professional forces, and the fiscal and industrial limitations on producing the kinds of munitions such forces would require if the United States mobilized. By the beginning of the 1980s there was a general agreement that U.S. conventional capability had dropped to dangerous levels. The continuing Soviet buildup, begun in the early 1970s and pursued relentlessly throughout the decade, had awakened concern throughout NATO, in general, and the United States, in particular. Especially disturbing were indications that for the first time the USSR was building a capability to move large forces quickly to destinations outside traditional Soviet spheres of activity. Soviet arms transfers, followed by advisers and, in some cases, by whole combat units into new areas, notably Angola and the Horn of Africa, gradually attracted the attention of the American public. Finally, the Soviet invasion of Afghanistan, the Iranian revolution, and subsequent events aroused popular support for a more vigorous defense program. The last defense budget submitted by President Jimmy Carter sharply increased military spending. The administration's proposal for the Rapid Deployment Force led perforce to an important and far-reaching examination of national mobilization and global deployment capabilities.

American defense was a central issue in the 1980 election. Writing in 1981, U.S. Representative Robin Beard pointed out that there was a "badly needed restructuring of the strategy and process whereby the United States procures its weapons. . . . Naval, air and strategic improvements are programmed at the expense of land warfare capabilities. Unless the incoming administration addresses this resource imbalance, the Army is destined to become an obsolete force by the end of this decade."[12] The present Chief of Staff of the U.S. Army has pointed out that "as recently as 1979 . . . much of our equipment reflected the technology of the 1960s, and the post-Vietnam defense funding reductions meant aging equipment fleets and shrinking inventories of weapons systems. The so-called short war strategy also took its toll as our staying power continued not to be funded adequately."[13]

As concern mounted over funding priorities, the army began searching in the early 1980s for a way to defeat the masses of Pact armor which it expected to meet on the European battlefield. Eventually an air-ground concept of blocking choke points and reducing vital Pact command and control facilities and formations deep in the enemy's rear was developed. If this could be done, the arrival of enemy armor on the battlefield could be prevented or delayed so that frontline battles could be fought on something like equal terms. This concept, called "Airland Battle" by the U.S. Army and Air Force, and "Follow-On Forces Attack" (FOFA) in a NATO variant, has been adopted by the U.S. forces and represents a decisive doctrinal step away from the quick war assumptions of the early 1970s. With the concepts embodied in Airland Battle, or FOFA, in place, American forces and NATO have an idea of how to fight an extended battle in Europe, with some prospect of success, although the strategic framework has not been amended: the blank wall after the early phase of hostilities still stands.

In an attempt to overcome shortages of strategic lift for U.S.-based reinforcements, the army in the late 1970s and early 1980s began to increase its stockpiles of combat-ready equipment and war stocks prepositioned in Europe. Funds allocated for materiel sustainability (the replacement of resources consumed or lost during combat) went from slightly over $5 billion in 1980 to around $14 billion projected for 1985.[14]

During the early and mid-1970s, 3 divisions' worth of mechanized and armored equipment had been maintained to equip "fly in" divisions deployed from the continental United States with only individual equipment.[15] Three more division sets have been committed to NATO and will be deployed by 1986. This program, called Prepositioned Overseas Materiel Configured in Unit Sets (POMCUS), will make possible the airlift to Europe of 6 armored or mechanized divisions within ten days of an order to deploy.[16]

In addition to forces prepositioned near the critical central front, the United States also has initiated a number of other programs designed to deliver forces rapidly to Europe in an emergency. The equipment for a marine amphibious brigade (MAB) is prepositioned in Norway. Considerable marine equipment and common munitions are prepositioned aboard a series of floating depot ships worldwide, oriented toward Southwest Asia but available elsewhere in an emergency. A number of fast roll-on, roll-off ships are being procured for sealift, and the Ready Reserve Fleet, consisting of vital break-bulk cargo ships, will be more than doubled in the next few years. Additional aerial tankers also are being obtained, and the Civil Reserve Air Fleet is being restructured. Freight haulers and transports will continuously compete against "glamor" items in the budget, but, however imperfectly, strategic mobility is coming into the light after years in the shadows.[17]

U.S. land forces that would take part in NATO defense fall generally into four groups. The first category consists of forces already stationed in Europe which would be immediately engaged by a Warsaw Pact or Soviet attack. Forward-deployed army forces, numbering about one-third of the total active army, consist of two corps (V and VII) which include 2 armored cavalry regiments, 2 armored divisions, 2 mechanized divisions, 1 armored brigade, and 1 mechanized brigade. One additional mechanized brigade is located in West Berlin, but it is not generally considered deployable to the central front in the event of war. These forward-deployed forces are maintained at combat readiness, the equivalent of Soviet Category 1. In addition there are numerous combat support, air defense, and logistic forces throughout the Federal Republic.

The second category of forces is active U.S. units stationed in the United States which have equipment in POMCUS. They presently consist of 1 additional corps headquarters (III Corps), 1 armored cavalry regiment, 2 armored divisions, 1 full mechanized division, and 1 mechanized division with 1 of 3 brigades already forward deployed. By 1986 another 2 divisions also will be POMCUS units. These forces would deploy rapidly to Europe by a combination of military airlift, the Civil Reserve Air Fleet, and possibly chartered commercial aircraft. A recent army initiative to restructure several infantry divisions into light divisions includes provision for at least 1 light division eventually to preposition equipment in Europe, in addition to the mechanized and armored divisions mentioned above.

The third category consists of active divisions, some with reserve "roundout" brigades, which would deploy with their equipment from the United States. This group includes a corps headquarters (XVIII Airborne), 2 mechanized divisions with 2 active brigades each, 2 infantry divisions with 2 active brigades each, 1 complete infantry division, 1 airborne division, 1 airmobile division, and 1 armored and 1 infantry brigade.[18] Two additional light infantry divisions are scheduled to be formed in the 1985–87 period as well, without adding to the army's total strength. Although their missions have not yet been formulated, at least one almost certainly will be assigned to reinforce Europe if required. From this pool also comes the army's forces for the Rapid Deployment Force, which currently numbers 4⅓ army divisions, plus a marine amphibious force (roughly a reinforced division with an air wing) and air force elements.[19] The army divisions—1 airborne, 1 air assault, 1 light, and 1 mechanized—are also dual-hatted for a NATO role; their availability will depend in large measure on which theater "cooks off" first.

In the fourth category are the National Guard and reserve forces which, by the end of 1985, had added 9 divisions (2 armored, 2 mechanized infantry, and 5 infantry); 26 brigades (4 armored, 9 mechanized, and 12 infantry, and the Alaskan 207th Infantry Group); and a large number of artillery, engineer, military police, signal, and other brigade-sized units.[20] Of this total, 1 brigade-sized unit is permanently deployed in Alaska, 1 in Hawaii is a roundout brigade for a Pacific-dedicated, 2-brigade active division, and 3 are roundouts for active divisions. As of 1984, 9 combat divisions (36 percent of all combat divisions) and two-thirds of the army's combat service support capability are in the reserve structure, plus the combat brigades mentioned above.[21] Also in the reserve system are 395,000 individual mobilization augmentees in the Individual Ready Reserves and the inactive National Guard who are trained soldiers with a continuing reserve commitment but who have not been assimilated into units. These former soldiers would play an important role as individual "fillers" to replace combat losses. The number in the IRR is planned to increase, but the end strength is not expected to meet army mobilization requirements.[22]

Finally, there is the draft pool, which in 1983–84 included roughly just over 2 million nineteen- to twenty-year-old males, less those already serving and some other categories. Previous year cohorts were holding above 2 million as well. Although no young men are presently being called up for active service, the United States is maintaining a system designed to provide inductees for training within 13 days of mobilization and about 280,000 within the first 60 days. Although preregistration is expected to save up to six weeks during a crisis, the earliest that draftees could be expected to arrive in units would be about 100 days after mobilization (M+100). Although peacetime registration is no guarantee of compliance with draft calls, it is a strong indicator that manpower would be available if needed. The current registration rate in the United States is about 93 percent of draft-age males.[23]

In addition to army forces the Marine Corps maintains 4 divisions of ground and air forces—3 regular and 1 reserve. One of the active duty divisions, with its air wing, is earmarked for deployment to NATO's northern flank if required, with the lead brigade falling in on the equipment prepositioned in Norway. The remaining 2 active division wing teams are oriented toward the Pacific theater. Although marine divisions are larger than army divisions, they are organized primarily as light infantry and lack the extended tactical mobility of mechanized or armored divisions. Marine units, from battalion up to division, can be quickly task-organized with their own organic air support. Being light, they can be rapidly deployed by transport aircraft as well as by amphibious shipping.

Setting aside the strategic bombardment role of the bomber and missile forces, the U.S. Air Force generally uses its air power in a theater role to support land objectives, as in World War II, or to mount an independent air campaign designed to assist indirectly the land campaign by interdicting enemy forces in the rear areas. U.S. naval air forces provide strike, antisubmarine, and fleet protection roles and in addition support forces ashore. Marine air wings are integral parts of marine divisions and are dedicated to the support of marine operations. In a discussion of NATO air power, the major American theater component comes from USAF tactical air forces.

American air power in the conventional theater role historically has been employed in three phases: achievement of air superiority, deep interdiction of enemy units to isolate the battlefield, and, finally, close air support of ground troops in the battle area itself. This pattern of employment of air power was learned in the Second World War and has been carried forward through the Korean and Vietnamese wars when enemy air forces were negligible, as in the case of Vietnam, or were swept from the skies and a comfortable margin of air superiority established fairly early in the battle, as in Korea. If war should come to the central front, however, these requirements would likely be telescoped together, which is the essence of the air force's dilemma in Airland Battle.

Like U.S. ground forces, American air forces also suffered during the post-Vietnam decline in funds and manpower, although the air force consistently has been the best recruited service among U.S. forces. In 1971 the total U.S. tactical air strength fell below that of the USSR.[24] For the air forces the period was especially difficult in a fiscal sense because the cost of replacing the aging F-4 fleet used by all services rose sharply as technology pushed aircraft performance and costs upward. The problem was exacerbated in the latter part of the decade by runaway inflation. One result of the tight budgets of the mid-1970s was a deliberate decision to buy additional aircraft at the expense of spare parts, munitions, and other readiness items in the hope that, by preserving force structure, readiness could be pulled along if a time should ever come when funds were available.[25] Inevitably this led to a decline in readiness and criticism from many fronts, including a group of military reformers who blamed U.S. aircraft design for being too complex and expensive. Even leaving the battles over strategic systems like the MX missile and the B-1 bomber aside, the 1970s were tough for U.S. tactical air forces. Despite constrained budgets, however, replacement of F-4s with F-15 air superiority fighters and F-16 multimission fighters was begun, and the A-10 close support aircraft, the first to be designed specifically for air-to-mud support of ground troops since World War II, began entering the inventory in significant numbers.

Evolution of the high-threat, short war doctrine by the ground forces affected the air forces in Europe primarily in terms of warning time and the shortage of air-to-air and air-to-ground munitions caused by budget deficiencies and procurement policies. The most likely air equivalent of the ground's Soviet-massed division attack is a massed Warsaw Pact air offensive of over 2,000 warplanes accompanied by electronic countermeasure aircraft blasting through the NATO air defense belt and attacking airfields, nuclear storage sites, command and control headquarters, and other targets. Like ground forces, allied air forces would have to fight outnumbered and win, a situation that is more critical because of the relatively narrow width of the Federal Republic and the proximity of sensitive targets to the IGB.

Beginning in the late 1970s and accelerating in the 1980s, the NATO air arm—Allied Air Forces Central Europe—has made improvements that will positively affect U.S. air power as part of NATO. Additional NATO E-3A airborne warning and control system aircraft are becoming available for enhanced early warning. Construction of aircraft shelters and service facilities will make bases more survivable and efficient so aircraft can be quickly turned around and relaunched. Airbase air defense also is being improved with the acquisition of more ground-mounted air defense systems, although the situation may not yet be fully satisfactory.[26] The acquisition of additional spare parts and flying hours is raising readiness throughout the service.

The transition from a short war doctrine to Airland Battle poses some cruel operational choices for the air force. The first is the emphasis on immediate deep interdiction even before air superiority has been gained. Since the bulk of U.S. combat aircraft is capable of performing both missions, and would be required in both, the allocation of missions per aircraft becomes critical. Attempting to strike deep before air superiority has been gained is likely to result in the loss of aircraft and crews that are also needed for air superiority missions. Second is the selection and control of deep interdiction targets. This is an easier problem to solve. Army and air force procedures are evolving to integrate more closely the targeting and mission allocations. There are still some doctrinal differences, but the trend is clearly toward more effective integration of the deep battle at the operational level.

There are other solutions on the horizon, principally the use of unmanned, slow-flying remotely piloted vehicles (RPV) to identify fixed and moving interdiction targets for artillery, aircraft, and missile strikes. "Smart" bombs, or even armed RPVs, can be effective against pinpoint targets that identify themselves, such as air defense radars and communications sites, but these are not likely to be effective against larger targets since they would have to be increased in size and cost. Likewise, conventional ground-to-ground ballistic missiles could be effective against Pact airfields and choke points like bridges and rail yards, thus aiding both the air superiority battle and the delay and disorganization of second echelon front forces. They would not, however, be effective against mobile targets. For the foreseeable future, manned aircraft will remain the delivery system that will be expected to accomplish the bulk of the deep interdiction called for in the U.S.—and NATO's—new doctrine.[27]

Before discussing actual forces a word should be said about naval air. The United States is alone in operating substantial numbers of fixed-wing fighter and interdiction aircraft from the sea. Although naval aircraft are primarily useful as naval weapons, they do have the capability of operating in land environments, particularly the A-6 all-weather attack aircraft. The numbers of aircraft per carrier would be relatively insignificant in the context of the massed formations expected to be employed at the beginning of a NATO conventional war, and the naval arm would be otherwise preoccupied. But, if the short war were protracted, assuming naval success and the expected attrition of land-based air on the central front, the impact of naval aviation, either carrier-launched or land-based, would increase dramatically, even considering the short "legs" of carrier-based air and the ability of aircraft carriers to stand in close to the battlefield and defend against, or absorb, air attack. Carrier vulnerability to land-based attack is an issue not likely to be settled by peacetime war games, and the admirals have an understandable reluctance to subscribe to the risk in advance. Still, carrier air represents a valuable resource once a European war scenario has played on long enough for attrition of NATO land-based air power to become a significant factor, which happens fairly quickly.[28]

The following figures attempt to count only those aircraft that are configured and could be used for air superiority, battlefield air interdiction, or close air support roles. They include combat aircraft in the training establishment of each service designated to be converted for operational attack of missions. In the following breakout, a *squadron* roughly consists of from 10 to 15 aircraft and a *wing* from 2 to 4 squadrons, depending on nationality.[29]

U.S. land-based air power, like ground forces, is partially deployed forward in NATO on a routine basis. Under U.S. Air Force, Europe there are 15 squadrons in Britain, 12 in Germany, 1 in the Netherlands, 1 in Iceland, and 3 in Spain of F-16 aircraft, with elements in Italy, Greece, and Turkey. Combat aircraft deployed forward consist of some 750 fighter and attack aircraft, with additional support aircraft deployed forward in smaller numbers. Carrier aircraft, which would be employed in the northern Atlantic and Mediterranean, consist of about 60 attack aircraft per carrier. There are normally 2 carriers within the NATO area, and at least 2 more could be deployed on short notice.

In the continental United States there are 15 fighter wings in the Tactical Air Command, which is responsible for reinforcing overseas commands in an emergency.[30] At least 1 tactical fighter wing is on call to reinforce Europe immediately, and other wings and squadrons can conduct transatlantic deployments on relatively short notice, given air-refueling assets and airlift to transport their support elements. Air reserves include the Air National Guard, with over 1,000 combat aircraft and the Air Force Reserve, flying about 188 combat aircraft. Generally, air reserve and guard units are considered nearly as capable as their active counterparts and would be deployed to Europe in a crisis.

Totals of combat aircraft available for a conventional war in Europe are difficult to pin down. Even the definition of "combat aircraft" is unclear, as totals usually do not count combat-capable aircraft in training squadrons and special mission aircraft like the MC-130 armed transport. In all, the *Military Balance* lists 1,893 combat strike aircraft in the active inventory which, along with the reserves, adds to over 3,100 attack aircraft (fighters capable of deep strike interdiction and, with the exception of FB-111 models, of air superiority operations, although the FB-111 is a potent runway buster). These figures do not include approximately 60 B-52 heavy bombers modified for a conventional role and hosts of support aircraft.

The numbers of naval strike aircraft which would be available to NATO are even more difficult to assess since their accessibility depends on ship deployments as well as on aircraft procurements. There are about 700 strike-capable aircraft normally available, 220 in the training base and about 110 in the naval reserve structure. The Marine Corps has approximately 330 active attack aircraft and an estimated 100 additional strike aircraft in reserve.

EUROPEAN NATO

From the neck of the Danish peninsula in the north to the Austrian border in the south, European NATO ground forces outnumber those of the United States along the 885-kilometer IGB that separates West Germany from East in the north and from Czechoslovakia in the south (see Map 2). A portion of West Germany north of Hamburg comes under the control of Commander, Allied Forces Northern Europe (ComAFNORTH) and would be defended with some German troops and Danish formations. The remainder of the front, virtually all of central

NATO's CENTRAL FRONT

Map 2.   Corps Sectors in NATO

Source: John M. Collins, *U.S.-Soviet Military Balance, 1960–1980* (Washington, DC: McGraw-Hill, 1980), p. 315. Reprinted by permission of John Collins and McGraw-Hill.

Europe, comes under the authority of Commander, Allied Forces Central Europe (ComAFCENT). Because of its size, AFCENT has been split into two: the Northern Army Group (NORTHAG) and the Central Army Group (CENTAG).

From the Danish boundary a West German corps is stationed in Schleswig-Holstein under AFNORTH, whose boundary with AFCENT runs roughly along the Elbe north of Bremerhaven near Hamburg. NORTHAG deploys 4 corps: 1 Dutch corps south of the Elbe, 1 West German corps, 1 British corps in the center of the North German Plain, and finally 1 Belgian corps along the border with CENTAG. The United States maintains a forward-deployed brigade of 1 U.S.-based armored division in the NORTHAG area where deploying units would fall in on prepositioned equipment. From the Belgian corps on his northern border, the CENTAG commander also deploys 4 corps: 1 West German corps, 2 U.S. corps, and 1 West German corps in the extreme south facing Czechoslovakia and Austria, which is neutral.

At full strength, and including American formations already discussed, NATO normally has about 21 divisions' worth of manpower in major combat units.[31] U.S. and West German forces tend to be the most fully prepared for combat, with other allied units requiring about three days to achieve wartime readiness.[32] With the exception of Britain, Canada, Luxembourg, and the United States, all other NATO countries which provide troops to central Europe—that is, all the continental powers—maintain reserve establishments, conscription, and have large pools of trained manpower.

THE CENTRAL FRONT: THE BIG THREE[33]

British ground forces include 3 armored divisions, 1 infantry division, 1 artillery division, and 22 brigades, with a total strength, including support, of 159,000. British forces, although small, are high quality and are deployed throughout the world. In an emergency, overseas commitments and gathering strength from scattered deployments would be considerations for the British as well as for the United States.

Britain is the only major European power to maintain an all-volunteer military establishment. Its forces are highly trained and thoroughly professional, and there is every indication they would fight very well on familiar terrain. Readiness in recent years has suffered, however, by periodic unit rotations to Northern Ireland and growing equipment obsolescence. The forces' main battle tank, *Chieftain*, was the first 120mm.-gunned tank in NATO, but it is now aging. An equipment upgrade is now under way, and the *Challenger* tank, a new infantry-fighting vehicle, and other items are due to enter the inventory, or are already doing so.

The Royal Air Force, with its *Harrier*, *Phantom*, and the newer *Toronado* aircraft, is very well trained; RAF pilots, like many of their NATO counterparts, use training facilities in Sardinia and the United States on a regular basis. Likewise, the Royal Navy is well practiced in its primarily antisubmarine role in the Atlantic and North seas and in the Channel.

British air forces muster about 620 combat aircraft, and air units supporting the BAOR can be reinforced in fairly quick order because of the short flight time from Britain to forward bases in Germany. It may be remembered that substantial U.S. air forces are maintained in Britain, including A-10 close support units that deploy, on order, to operational fields within the Federal Republic.

The British Army of the Rhine (BAOR), deployed in West Germany, consists of 3 armored divisions plus supporting elements. In an emergency, reinforcements for the BAOR include 4 infantry brigades (2 regular and 2 Territorial Army), the United Kingdom Mobile Force of 1 infantry brigade plus support, and other smaller combat and combat support units.

British naval forces would provide valuable antisubmarine service on the northern approaches to Europe; for that reason Britain's naval organization stresses the antisubmarine role. The Royal Navy sails 25 submarines (12 nuclear), 3 ASW carriers, and about 60 destroyers and frigates, plus assorted patrol, amphibious and mine-countermeasure craft. There also ballistic missile submarines, but these will not be considered here.

In numbers, France's armed forces are only slightly behind those of the Federal Republic—492,850 to 495,000. In addition to substantial conventional forces, France operates an independent nuclear force, including tactical missiles and 46 *Pluton* tactical nuclear missiles that are roughly comparable to the U.S. *Lance* missile and would be deployed in support of

French field units. The French nuclear "wild card" must loom large in Warsaw Pact, which is to say Soviet, calculations of the force balance in Europe. The French Republic keeps its own nuclear counsel.

French forces are capable and trained to high standards, which tend to emphasize small unit tactics, and soldiers are routinely exposed to commando-style training in specialized areas. Some equipment, primarily armored-fighting vehicles, is obsolescent, and armor and artillery designs seem to emphasize speed over armored protection and firepower, resulting in undergunned tanks (105mm. versus 120mm.) and artillery (mixed 105mm. and 155mm. versus 122mm. and 203mm.). Some improvement in artillery is under way. The result is ground forces better suited for overseas power projection than for fighting Pact forces in Europe. Still, as one observer told the author, the French are "damned tough" and would probably do well, even considering equipment limitations.

Current ground forces include 8 armored divisions, each roughly one-half the size of a U.S. armored division; 4 motorized rifle divisions; 1 Alpine division of 2 regiments; and 1 Quick Reaction Force consisting of 1 parachute division, 1 air-portable marine division, 1 light brigade, and support. A pending reorganization will reconfigure the QRF into an autonomous Rapid Action Force comprised of a marine, airborne, and alpine division, as well as 2 new divisions, 1 airmobile, and 1 light armored. In addition, existing forces will transition from 8 armored divisions and 4 motorized to 6 larger armored divisions, 2 motorized divisions, and 2 cadred armored cavalry brigades.[34]

Three armored divisions are deployed to southern Germany, although they are not under NATO command. Their reaction to a Warsaw Pact attack, however, is assumed to favor NATO. "Albeit the French forces do not form part of the integrated military defense organization of the North Atlantic Alliance, France has never left any doubt that she would honor her commitments to the Alliance in the event of a military conflict; her forces are already contributing to overall deterrence."[35]

Air power includes naval carrier-based air as well as conventional ground squadrons. There are about 550 ground-based combat aircraft and 167 naval combat aircraft. Training and expertise are high, although pilot flying hours have been cut back.

The French navy employs 2 conventional aircraft carriers, 18 attack submarines (1 nuclear), 1 cruiser, 45 destroyers and frigates, and a large number of smaller craft. Naval forces are also well trained and in wartime could contribute greatly to the security of the Mediterranean. France's tendency to see its European commitments as part of a larger global view has had an effect on naval orientation. Although slightly smaller in manpower than the Royal Navy, the French fleet's organization tends more toward a power-projection/intervention force than an antisubmarine/defensive force, the best examples of which are its aircraft carriers.

The Federal Republic of Germany maintains the largest, best equipped, and most powerful army in Europe. Training standards are high, equipment is new, and the active field forces are backed by an efficient conscription and a reserve force that frees field units for combat. West Germany's training areas are cramped, and, to compensate, the *Bundeswehr* trains ground forces in France, Wales, and Canada. Its main battle tank, *Leopard II,* is equivalent to the U.S. M-1 and probably superior to any armor fielded by the Pact. There are a number of armored-fighting vehicles, ranging from *Marder,* which was introduced some years ago and is still among the best in the world today, to obsolescent U.S. M-113s.

The land power of the Federal Republic's *Bundeswehr* is divided into the Field Army, which is comprised of the major maneuver forces, and the Territorial Army, the duty of which is largely rear-area security. The Field Army consists of 6 armored divisions, 4 armored infantry divisions, 1 mountain division, and 1 airborne division. (At 17,000 men a West German armored division is slightly smaller than its 18,000+ U.S. counterpart.) West German divisions are heavier than any other NATO formations except U.S. units.

The Territorial Army is composed of 6 heavy home-guard brigades, each with 2 tank and 2 infantry battalions and 1 artillery battalion manned in peacetime at various strengths, ranging from 85 to 52 percent, and filled out on mobilization by reservists. The home-guard heavy brigades are tasked with reinforcing NATO formations employed in forward positions as well as security in the rear areas.[36] These 6 formations recently have been made available to NATO, while the remainder of the Territorial Army is still under West German national control.[37]

There are 6 lighter home-guard brigades with 1 tank, 2 infantry battalions, and 1 artillery battalion, all of which are weapons storage units in peacetime. After the brigades, there are 15 home-guard regiments, consisting of 45 home-guard battalions of motorized infantry, plus 150 home-guard companies and about 300 security platoons for point security in the rear areas. (In peacetime they serve as weapons holding units.[38]) An additional 6 Territorial Army brigades are to be raised as regional reserve units.[39] Finally, behind the organized reserves, there are about 500,000 other reservists, or prior servicemen not organized into units but who are trained soldiers available as fillers to replace losses on fairly short notice. While these personnel do not represent an organized military capability, they are very significant in terms of total defense.[40]

The air force's Tactical Command disposes of about 470 aircraft; the Naval Air Arm provides an additional 120 land-based planes, for an estimated total of 590 fighters and attack aircraft. Aircrew training is excellent, and German aviators, especially fighter pilots, train extensively at German bases in the United States, for example, those located at Fort Bliss and Luke. The navy sails 24 diesel submarines, 14 destroyers and frigates, 6 corvettes, and a large number of fast attack craft, patrol boats, coastal minesweepers, and assorted support craft. Oriented primarily toward the Baltic and North seas, German naval forces, especially submarines, receive high marks from U.S. naval personnel.

THE OTHER NATO POWERS

Belgium maintains 2 divisions of armored and mechanized infantry, plus assorted light infantry brigades and some battalions. Less than one-half of its active armed forces is deployed forward in Germany, making deployment extremely dependent on early warning; even the forward-deployed forces are stationed long distances from their wartime positions. The time required to move Belgian and Dutch forces to their defensive positions might well be the "pacing factor" that drives

NATO mobilization deadlines. Equipment procurement has been hampered by funding restrictions, thereby resulting in obsolescence; for example, the main battle tank remains the *Leopard I*, and there are no plans for further procurement. Equipment availability is low because of spare part shortages. Artillery is very inadequate, consisting only of 2 active 155mm. self-propelled, or track-mounted, battalions and 1 203mm. self-propelled battalion. There also is a reserve battalion with towed 203mm. howitzers.

Belgian air forces consist of 144 combat aircraft, including new F-16s that are replacing older airframes. Pilot flying time has been reduced below NATO's required fifteen-hour-per-month minimum, which will adversely affect readiness. Further, Belgium has announced disbandment of a number of its ground-to-air missile squadrons, thereby jeopardizing the integrity of NATO's air defense belt. Naval forces possess 4 frigates and an assortment of smaller craft, notably mine countermeasures and minesweeper vessels that would be invaluable for sweeping operations along the North Sea littoral.

Canada maintains a mechanized brigade group of 3,200 in West Germany and 2 brigade groups in Canada of mixed types of combat units. The training and readiness standards of the Canadian all-volunteer force are excellent; however, it is so small, and its equipment so obsolescent, that the brigade group would not play a significant role in the central front battle. Canada's main battle tank remains the *Leopard I*, and its armored-fighting vehicle is the outdated U.S. M-113. While the present Canadian force structure reflects a previous lack of political commitment to stronger defense, the election of the Conservative government in Canada may in time rectify some of the brigade's most serious shortcomings.

Air forces consist of about 100 combat aircraft. Of these, 42 CF-104s are stationed in Germany and are to be replaced with 54 CF-18s. Pilots are well trained in air-to-ground operations, but readiness suffers from obsolescent equipment. Naval forces include 3 diesel submarines, 20 active destroyers, and assorted small craft.

Denmark's ground forces consist of 5 mechanized infantry brigades and 5 light regimental combat teams. In case of war the single Danish division would defend in Schleswig-Holstein in cooperation with West German forces. Although Denmark has an extensive mobilization system, equipment is obsolescent, and training and readiness standards are reported to be mediocre.[41] Denmark's unique geographical circumstance makes it particularly vulnerable to attack by air, airborne, and seaborne forces, and it would probably be dependent on allied reinforcement to defend itself. Danish forces are not deployed forward in Germany in peacetime.

Like Belgium and other European powers, Denmark relies heavily on reserve forces to flesh out regular units. Reserves consist of an immediate Augmentation Force of 6,000 for deployment into defensive positions in Germany; a Field Army Reserve of 45,000, designed to bring regular units to war strength and to add a mechanized battalion to each brigade; a Regional Defense Force of 24,000, to be organized into 7 regimental combat teams; and an Army Home Guard of 60,400. In addition, there are about 30,000 other reservists and home guards.[42] Denmark's air forces fly around 116 combat aircraft, and its naval forces sail 5 diesel submarines, 5 frigates, 5 fishery-protection frigates, and a number of coastal patrol craft.

Italy's ground forces include 1 armored division, 3 mechanized divisions, and 11 independent brigades of various types. In addition to regular forces, the *Carabinieri* mount a mechanized brigade, with 13 battalions, 1 airborne battalion, and 2 cavalry squadrons, plus smaller internal security units. The Italian air force flies 300 combat aircraft. Its sea power is provided by 10 diesel submarines, 1 helicopter carrier, 2 cruisers, 15 destroyers and frigates, and a large number of corvettes and fast attack craft, ocean and coastal minesweepers, and support vessels.

Active army forces in the Netherlands consist of 2 armored brigades and 4 mechanized infantry brigades, with an additional 4 brigades (1 tank, 2 mechanized infantry, and 1 infantry) and support troops in the reserves. An armored brigade is maintained forward in West Germany, covering a corps sector and making the defense of the Dutch sector, like the Belgian, dependent on early mobilization and deployment of forces forward.

Equipment in the Dutch ground forces is generally modern; over 100 *Leopard II*s are in service, the 450+ *Leopard I* tank fleet is being upgraded, and more *Leopard II*s have been ordered to replace the obsolescent *Centurions* still in use. A new armored-fighting vehicle is being issued and training is good. The air force has 182 combat aircraft and is buying

F-16s for air-to-ground support. The navy consists of 6 submarines, 23 destroyers, frigates, and corvettes, as well as a number of coastal minesweepers and patrol craft.

THE NORTHERN FLANK

Because of its strategic implications for the central front battle, the defense of NATO's northern flank has an immediate impact on the success of the defense of central Europe. Norway has a brigade group of 2 infantry battalions and 1 tank company in northern Norway, 1 reinforced battalion in southern Norway, and some independent armored squadrons and infantry battalions. The reserves count 12 regimental combat teams of about 5,000 men each. There is also an Army Home Guard of 81,500, plus 16,000 in the naval reserves.

Norway's unique geography virtually dictates concentration on small unit operations since only perhaps in the Finnmark region in northern Norway could even division-scaled armored operations be practical. Norwegian equipment is generally old; the main battle tank is the *Leopard I* and a number of modified U.S. M-48 models. Concentration in training is on home-guard operations and in defense missions to the north. Air power consists of 115 combat aircraft, including newer F-16s. Naval forces count 14 diesel submarines, 5 frigates, 2 corvettes, and a number of patrol and minesweeper craft.

THE SOUTHERN FLANK

Greece and Turkey anchor NATO in the south. Both are Mediterranean powers that offer an approach to the Warsaw Pact "underbody" through Bulgaria, the Black Sea, and the Caucasus. The two countries spend above the NATO average of percentage of GNP on arms. Unfortunately, they arm primarily against each other. Equipment tends to be old and obsolescent; main battle tanks for each country are the *Leopard I*, U.S. M-48, and older models.

Rugged typography and geographical position compensate for equipment and terrain shortfalls. From their positions on the flank, both countries would constitute areas of secondary interest to the Pact should war with NATO erupt. Mountains along the borders and limited avenues of approach would multiply the worth of even obsolescent equipment in the defense.

Turkey's guardianship of the Bosporus is essential to "bottling up" the Soviet Black Sea Fleet and preventing a Soviet end run into the Mediterranean, either by naval, air, or land forces, or by preventing a land linkup between the Soviets and Iraq or Syria. Like Turkey, Greece secures a vital segment of the Mediterranean littoral. The continued neutrality of Yugoslavia and Albania is more secure with democratic Greece to their south. The Greek isles offer havens for U.S. and other NATO naval forces, basing for air power striking up through Bulgaria and Romania toward the Kiev and Odessa military districts and indirectly assisting NATO in a central front battle by pinning down Pact resources in the south.

The combined forces of Greece and Turkey consist of about 30 divisions and over 25 independent brigades, plus large reserves of manpower and over 620 combat aircraft. While the majority of land divisions is light infantry and not all the combat aircraft are modern, there should be adequate forces to defend themselves against a Pact attack, assuming that sufficient war stocks are available to maintain the fight. Furthermore, the navies of the two countries add up to an impressive capability to patrol the closed and crowded seas of the eastern Mediterranean.

COMMAND STYLE

Counts of men and materiel, and even training assessments, give an incomplete picture of an army or an alliance's ability to wage war. Armies are essentially reflections of the societies from which they spring; strategies, in a distant way, reflect the "command styles" of the soldiers who plan them, and those styles grow from the corporate military experience of a particular country. Professional military men overwhelmingly agree that indefinables—spirit, courage, resourcefulness—mean more than mere numbers of tanks or artillery pieces. The best expression of this is perhaps a comment by de Saxe that "it is not the big armies that win battles; it is the good ones." The making of a "good" army seems to rest historically on a number of things, among which is the degree of leadership and initiative shown at all levels, from top to bottom, from supreme command to the individual soldier.

The command style of the major Western armies is to give only general instructions, which the military calls "mission orders," to subordinates and to allow them maximum freedom in interpretation and execution. For example, a divisional commander will define for both his brigade or regimental subordinates only an objective, general concept, zone of action, or such minimum control measures as are necessary to coordinate their actions. The means and manner by which they maneuver their forces to accomplish the division's goals are their own responsibilities. The U.S. Army's premier field manual, *FM 100-5, Operations*, spells out the American version:

> Mission orders require commanders to determine *intent*—what they want to happen to the enemy. . . . While detailed orders may be necessary at times, commanders must trust their subordinates to make correct on-the-spot decisions within the mission framework. . . . Mission orders need only cover three important points:
> —They should clearly state the commander's objective, what he wants done, and why he wants it done.
> —They should establish limits or controls necessary for coordination.
> —They should delineate the available resources and support from outside sources.
> . . . if the battle develops so that previously issued orders no longer fit the new circumstances, the subordinate must inform his commander and propose appropriate alternatives. If this is not possible, *he must act as he knows his commander would and make a report as soon as possible.*[43]

The conscious objective of such a system is, or should be, the fostering of individual initiative in every leader so that sudden battlefield opportunities can be intelligently acted upon without delay. This kind of command philosophy, if accompanied by sound doctrine and professional skill, leads to a maneuver-oriented style of warfare which responds quickly to changing situations and opportunities. To a degree the style shows up in military organizations, notably in the French in their preference for small, maneuverable divisions and lightly armored and gunned vehicles with superior mobility. It demands much from its leadership: thought, initiative, and versatility as well as a kind of independence and risk-taking that perhaps runs counter to popular perceptions of military behavior.[44] On the central front, in the face of the shock of battle, lost communications, and general confusion, the side that can best react to changing situations will have a decided advantage, perhaps even offsetting to a degree deficiencies in numbers. This type of general orientation exists today in Western armies; Soviet and Pact style is radically different and will be discussed in Chapter Three.

CONCLUSIONS

According to NATO, its member nations support 4.4 million personnel on active military service, of which 2.6 million are in Europe. When France is added the total rises to about 3 million. The Warsaw Pact has 5.7 million personnel under arms, of which 4 million are in Europe facing NATO. Both NATO and the Pact are heavily dependent on mobilization to achieve full wartime capability, but, when reserve forces are added on anything like equal or slightly less than equal mobilization terms for the West, the essential balance remains unchanged for the mid-term and favors the West in the long (60+ days) term. The problem of NATO defense is not a shortage of people.

The picture that emerges from an examination of NATO's armies is one of a force that requires some degree of warning and mobilization but which can stand to arms fairly quickly, once the decision is made, and fight under leaders schooled in maneuver and initiative. Virtually all the European NATO countries maintain large reserve establishments (see Table 1), and the model for the most part is of reservists already integrated into units, mobilizing on or near terrain they will ultimately defend. Not all of those factors are under NATO control, and therefore not all appear in NATO strength counts.

Analysts at the Brookings Institution, in a study of NATO conventional defense, claim that after four days of mobilization NATO could in fact field over 30 divisions and after nine

Table 1. Selected European Reserve Establishments

Country	Strength	Units	Other Reservists
Belgium	160,000	2 bdes 11 home grd rgts	28,000
Britain	219,642	2 bdes 5 cav rgts 35 (+) bns	64,821
France	305,000	13 inf divs 23 terr inf rgts	88,000
Netherlands	145,000	1 armd bde 2 mech bdes 1 light inf bde 2 (+) home grd bdes	26,000
West Germany	755,000*	12 home grd bdes 15 (+) home grd rgts	

*Figure includes all services.
Sources: Adapted from John D. Steinbruner and Leon V. Segal, eds., *Alliance Security: NATO and the No-First-Use Question* (Washington, DC: Brookings Institution, 1983), p. 62; and International Institute for Strategic Studies, *The Military Balance, 1984–1985* (London: IISS, 1984), pp. 31–41.

days 43. Neither the Brookings study nor the NATO figures includes the various home-guard organizations that would be mostly concerned with security in the rear areas and also could provide manpower fillers into frontline units or fight, if necessary, on the defensive on home ground and protect their own supply points. The quality of all these units varies, but, given the differences between the size of smaller Soviet-style divisions and Western ones, the numbers of attackers to defenders across NATO's front do not seem favorable for a decisive Pact breakthrough.

Notes

[1] Collins, *Military Balance*, p. 316.
[2] Federal minister of defense, *White Paper 1979: The Security of the Federal Republic of Germany and the Development of Federal Armed Forces* (Bonn: Ministry of Defense, 1979), p. 126.

³Collins, *Military Balance*, p. 89n. The data on the breakout of category 1, 2, and 3 divisions are from *Military Balance, 1983–1984;* and William P. Mako, *U.S. Ground Forces and the Defense of Central Europe* (Washington, DC: Brookings Institution, 1983), Table 3–2, p. 44.

⁴The United States has moved toward a greater reliance on reserve forces. By 1989, 51 percent of U.S. forces will be in the reserve structure. See Lawrence J. Korb, "The Major Elements of Force Mix Decisions," *Defense '84* (April 1984): 18.

⁵Collins, *Military Balance*, pp. 182–89.

⁶Ibid., p. 580.

⁷The size of combatant units did not go down. A U.S. tank division numbered 10,670 in 1945, compared to 18,000 in 1980, despite the fact that tank gun effectiveness has about doubled. The army's present drive to lighten units may reverse this trend.

⁸*Operations* (1976), p. 1–1 (emphasis in original).

⁹In the U.S. structure the difference between mechanized or armored divisions is slight, being provided by a mix favoring mechanized battalions in the infantry divisions and tanks in the armored divisions. The proportions are generally 2 mechanized infantry brigades to 1 armor in the infantry divisions, versus 2 armored brigades to 1 infantry in the armored divisions. Brigades are usually 3 or 4 battalions, with the mix being about two-thirds tank or infantry. Tank or mechanized infantry battalions are the same in either type division.

Since brigades cross attach freely in organizing for combat, the methods of operation are nearly the same, with a slight edge to the armored divisions in offensive operations. Divisional artillery support, which is organic to either division, remains the same.

¹⁰Collins, *Military Balance*, pp. 511, 531, 535.

¹¹The author learned the lesson the hard way as a planner in the early days of the Rapid Deployment Joint Task Force. This point has been mentioned in many studies. Collins addresses it in *Military Balance*, pp. 271–72.

¹²Robin Beard, "Agenda for Defense: A Congressional Perspective," *Strategic Review* 9, no. 1 (Winter 1981): 10, 12.

¹³John A. Wickham, Jr., "Reinforcing and Strengthening the Conventional Defense," *NATO's Sixteen Nations*, Special No. 1, vol. 28, no. 5 (1983): 93.

¹⁴Caspar W. Weinberger, *Annual Report to the Congress: Fiscal Year 1984* (Washington, DC: Government Printing Office, 1983), pp. 227, 231 (hereafter cited as *DoD 1984 Budget*).

¹⁵This is a slight oversimplification. Such divisions have some rolling stock and aircraft that require heavy lift transports, but the essential divisional fighting formations are lifted with only hand-carried gear.

¹⁶*DoD 1984 Budget*, p. 212.

¹⁷Ibid., p. 209.

¹⁸Ibid., pp. 217–18.

¹⁹Mako, *U.S. Ground Forces*, p. 51. The exact composition of this category is subject to change as the U.S. Army designates the two POMCUS divisions and carries through a recently announced organizational change of some of the remaining divisions in this grouping to light infantry.

²⁰Association of the U.S. Army, *Army Green Book 1983–84: Status Report on Landpower* 33, no. 10 (1983): 272–74. See also an information booklet by the director of the Army Budget, entitled *The Army Budget: FY 1985*, pp. 15–18.

²¹Department of the Army, *Posture of the Army and Department of the Army Budget Estimates for Fiscal Year 1984* (Washington, DC: Government Printing Office, 1983), p. 57.

²²*DoD 1984 Budget*, p. 104.

²³Herbert C. Puschek, "Selective Service Registration: Success or Failure?" *Armed Forces and Society* 10, no. 1 (Fall 1983): 7–9, 22.

²⁴Robert N. Ginsburgh, "The United States Air Force," in Ray Bonds, ed., *The U.S. War Machine* (New York: Crown, 1978), p. 152.

[25] Beard, "Agenda for Defense," p. 11.

[26] Benjamin F. Schemmer, "We Can Count on Our Allies; I'm Not Sure the Warsaw Pact Can Count on Theirs," *Armed Forces Journal* 119, no. 5 (January 1982): 26.

[27] K. Peter Stratmann, "Prospective Tasks and Capabilities Required for NATO's Conventional Forces," in ESS, *Strengthening Conventional Deterrence in Europe*, pp. 181–83.

[28] Author's observations in several naval war games, during which senior naval officers have attempted to come to grips with maneuvering carriers to support land campaigns on the central front.

[29] Unless cited otherwise, figures are from *Military Balance, 1983–1984*.

[30] Ginsburgh, "United States Air Force," p. 152.

[31] Mako, *U.S. Ground Forces*, p. 48.

[32] Ibid.

[33] The following data are drawn from a number of sources, chief among which is *Military Balance, 1983–1984*.

[34] Diego A. Ruiz Palmer, "The Front Line in Europe: National Contributions," *Armed Forces Journal* 121, no. 10 (May 1984): 61.

[35] *1979 White Paper*, p. 118. The West Germans' confidence in French reaction, contrasted with a U.S. tendency to discount France as a major force on the central front, is an example of how even close allies' perspectives can differ.

[36] Federal minister of defense, *White Paper 1983: The Security of the Federal Republic of Germany and the Development of Federal Armed Forces* (Bonn: Ministry of Defense, 1983), pp. 124–25.

[37] Ibid.

[38] *White Paper 1979*, p. 156.

[39] *White Paper 1983*, p. 124.

[40] Mako, *U.S. Ground Forces*, Table 4–1, p. 89.

[41] Ruiz Palmer, "The Front Line in Europe," p. 61.

[42] Unless otherwise noted, figures are from *The Military Balance, 1984–1985* (London: IISS, 1984). A weakness of this chart is that it does not reflect the pool of trained former soldiers who have finished active reserve obligations.

[43] U.S. Army, *FM 100-5, Operations* (Washington, DC: Government Printing Office, 1982), p. 2–7 [hereafter cited as *Operations* (1982)]. Author's emphasis. This is the current edition that replaced the 1976 version. The newer manual restores emphasis on the offensive, which many officers believed was a defect of the earlier publication.

[44] "A major, receiving a tongue-lashing from the Prince for a tactical blunder, offered the excuse that he had been obeying orders, and reminded the Prince that a Prussian officer was taught that an order from a superior was tantamount to an order from the King. Frederick Charles promptly responded: 'His Majesty made you a major because he believed you would know when *not* to obey his orders.' This simple story became guidance for all future generations of German officers." Trevor N. Dupuy, *A Genius for War: The German Army and General Staff, 1807–1945* (Englewood Cliffs, NJ: Prentice-Hall, 1977), p. 116.

Chapter Three

The Soviets and the Warsaw Pact

SOVIET STRATEGY

THE PRIMARY AIM of Soviet military policy and strategy is security. The maintenance of large and modern forces to protect the Soviet Union from outside threats enjoys broad support in the USSR, where military power is woven much more tightly into the tapestry of everyday domestic and external affairs than in the West. Soviet military forces, including KGB troops, sometimes play an active role in maintaining internal security. Soviet military power is the medium in which patriotism and the Communist system are mixed.[1] Externally, the Soviets see themselves threatened from every side; to them, security only can be guaranteed by maintaining strength equal to the sum of all their potential enemies. "The Soviet Union has to maintain not only the general balance of forces above all between the USSR and the United States, and between the Warsaw Pact and NATO, but also the regional equilibrium in individual directions which, militarily, have all peculiarities of their own."[2]

To understand the strategy and doctrines of the Soviet Union and its allies, at least a passing look is necessary at the historic, social, and economic context of the Soviet military view since that view is fundamental to the way the Soviets plan and assess risks to themselves. How the USSR became such a nationalized, militaristic society is especially puzzling when one reflects that the original Communist Revolution in Russia, according to Lenin's blueprint, was the beginning of a truly international movement. Marx and Lenin both believed that nationalism was doomed, but the contradiction of Russia can be seen today, with its deliberate and pervasive glorification of Mother Russia, the sacrifices of the Great Patriotic War, and its huge armed forces deployed on explicitly nationalistic terms.

Historically, Russia has seen itself as a land besieged. From the earliest settlement around the Moskva River, the Belorussian and Great Russian peoples were surrounded by other races: the Kazaks and Tatars to the south and east and the Poles and Danes and Livonian Knights to the west. There were no natural defenses, only the thinly populated broad plains and steppes. The Russian solution was expansion, a course which the czars pursued so successfully between the 1500s and 1917 that Russia grew from a small kingdom, set uncertainly between east and west, to an empire that stretched from Poland, and often including Poland, to the Pacific.

This chronic feeling of insecurity was abetted by a sense of being shut out of Europe. Rudyard Kipling's comment that a Russian is an Oriental with his shirt tucked in was rooted in a general European belief that Russia, if not quite Mongol, was not quite European either. Social and economic backwardness played a role: when the Industrial Revolution took off in western Europe, Russia lagged behind. Despite the efforts of several czars, prerevolution Russia never managed to develop the educated, middle-class infrastructure of managers so essential to a modern state and to modern armies. By sheer size, Russia ranked among the world's great military powers, but size only counted on the defensive. When Russian forces met the armies and navies of modern states in offensive war, their performance was usually poor, as for example in the initial battles against Napoleon, the Japanese in the Russo-Japanese War, and the Germans in two world wars. Only when overwhelming mass could be applied against an enemy already worn down by distance were Russian arms successful. Edward Luttwak has described this traditional pattern of Soviet strategy:

> When the poverty of Russian management, tactical rigidity and the vast distances that had to be crossed to come to grips with an enemy are taken together, the great disparity between Russia's strength in defeating invasion and her own weakness in offensive operations is sufficiently explained. . . . On the defensive, Russia would always ultimately defeat her enemy—then advance to drive the invader out, and finally to advance in turn, making easy conquests against armies already defeated.[3]

Thus the Russian revolutionaries inherited a strategic tradition that required no radical changes in the early years of social experimentation. The kinds of armies Lenin and Trotsky built reflected the priorities of the new Communist state. After a period of experimenting with rankless units, they reverted to more traditional forms, but the Russian emphasis on mass remained, and, as a result of the kind of society that began forming, the class of military "middle managers" who interpret and execute orders in Western countries never really got established in the Red Army. A mass army—one that can cover its mistakes by sending in still more troops—can afford this kind of strategy so long as it is employed in a theater where mass can be brought to bear. This is consistent with the history of the armies of the czars, and it is likewise consistent with the history of the Red Army through Afghanistan. Every time the Russians have successfully engaged a first-class enemy, they have only succeeded by applying overwhelming land power and only after exhausting the enemy by prolonged defense.

There are useful lessons in Russian history of how an army that prefers mass and springs from a regimented, oppressive society performs on the battlefield. A former German officer, with extensive combat experience against the Russians in World War II, gives the individual Soviet soldier high marks for toughness and courage, but he adds:

> . . . the Russians launched attacks with almost proverbial inflexibility, although at times their tank formations offered striking exceptions. The incredibly repetitive attacks at the same spot, the inflexibility of Russian artillery fire, and the choice of similar terrain for attacks betrayed a lack of imagination, reflection and mental agility. German listening posts often heard the frantic question 'What do we do now?' In the German experience few of the junior and middle rank Russian commanders demonstrated independent judgement when faced with either unexpected setbacks or opportunities for exploitation.[4]

Although von Mellenthin's experience is now forty years old, indications are that Soviet command style has not appreciably changed. Such a force tends to be doubly oppressive of its own soldiers, discourages initiative, and encourages buckpassing. From defectors and thousands of legal emigrants who are former Red Army soldiers and airmen comes a dismal picture of life in the army of a totalitarian state. Viktor Suvorov, a former Soviet officer of fifteen years' service, commanded a tank company during the invasion of Czechoslovakia in 1968 and was a staff officer and a student at the elite Frunze Military Academy. He has pictured life at the troop level as unrelieved hardship, cynicism, and boredom. Suvorov writes that, "if war with the West should break out, Soviet soldiers would surrender by the million. . . . The Politburo has no illusions about this."[5] Even allowing for Suvorov's optimism, his view of life in the barracks and the lack of initiative and authority at lower levels match generally with that brought out by other former soldiers and are military considerations that, while they should not be taken too optimistically, they should not be ignored. As Luttwak has pointed out, armies with those characteristics are more useful on the defense, where one only has to stand and fight, than in offensive, fluid situations where personal initiative and leadership count at all ranks. In a preprogrammed offensive, initiative and decentralization would have relatively low value, but preprogramming is difficult in maneuvers and impossible in war. Clausewitz wrote:

> Everything in war is very simple, but the simplest thing is difficult. The difficulties accumulate and end by producing a kind of friction that is inconceivable unless one has experienced war. . . . Countless minor incidents—the kind you can never really foresee—combine to lower the general level of performance, so that one always falls short of the intended goal. Iron will-power can overcome this friction; it pulverizes every obstacle, but of course it wears down the machine as well.[6]

The neutralization of NATO is a primary Soviet foreign policy objective. Given the risks posed by a war on the Continent, the Kremlin leadership would greatly prefer that neutralization be peaceful. This would be accomplished first by politically separating the United States from Europe and then by eroding European will to resist Soviet hegemony in the long term. This can best be done, the Soviets believe, by economic and political policies that exacerbate rifts in the Western Alliance and encourage or support groups that undermine political consensus in the democracies, such as the unilateral nuclear disarmament groups and various other lobbies, and by active economic and political pressures against existing governments. In keeping with the long view of history taken by Communists, this course is correct because it does not seriously endanger the gains made thus far by Communist states. It also conforms to the cautious nature that the bureaucratic Soviets normally show.

Taking the long view in recent times, however, must give the Soviet Union little reason for confidence. The economic well-being and vigorous natures of the European democracies, in contrast to that of the Soviet Union, and the rising expectations and liberal outlooks of the Eastern bloc countries, hardly forecast the eventual success of communism. Things are better in the West, and the East knows it (see Table 2).

The USSR's response since the latter stages of the Khrushchev period has been an increasing militarization of its own society and of its methods to affect change on the world scene. The Soviets' huge buildup since the late 1960s is more than just a reaction to Western arms, although surely reaction was an element in their calculations. The growth of Soviet military power has to be seen in the context of a Soviet grand strategy which combines all the elements of national power to achieve Soviet goals worldwide. The fact that the USSR has leaned more and more toward military means to spread influence, including the sponsorship and support of terrorism, since "revolutionary strategy" is a legitimate and original Communist invention, is an uneasy confirmation that the Kremlin

Table 2. Estimated Rates of Growth of Soviet GNP and Selected Subdivisions

	1955–60	1960–65	1965–70	1970–75	1980
GNP	6.0	4.9	5.4	3.7	1.4
Origin					
Agriculture	4.1	2.4	4.2	−2.1	−4.4
Construction	10.9	5.1	5.5	5.3	2.5
Transportation	10.8	8.2	7.5	6.6	3.3
Use					
Consumption	5.3	4.0	5.0	3.7	2.2
New Fixed Investment	10.4	6.6	6.3	4.7	2.3
Capital Repair	10.3	8.2	6.1	9.1	4.6

Source: Herbert Block, "The Economic Basis of Soviet Power," in Edward N. Luttwak, *The Grand Strategy of the Soviet Union* (New York: St. Martin's Press, 1983), Table 5, p. 171. Reprinted by permission of St. Martin's Press and Weidenfeld and Nicolson (London).

believes itself increasingly unable to use worldwide the political or economic legs of grand strategy. All the world's a stage for Soviet maneuvering; Europe, however, because of its central position to the Soviet Union and the West, is a special case.

The Kremlin has shown a cautious willingness to use military power in instances not directly related to the security of the USSR and when there was a clear advantage in doing so. For example, the Soviets are willing to take limited military risks in the Third World, with the continuing deployment of their technicians and advisers in Latin America and Syria. It is unclear and largely irrelevant whether they see this use of power as fulfilling their duties as good Marxists-Leninists, or whether they are simply asserting their prerogatives, as they perceive them, as a superpower. Perhaps they themselves do not make the distinction. But this ability and willingness to use power overseas, and to engage in the calculations and risks of military or quasimilitary operations in an unstable world, reveal Soviet pragmatism and sophistication involving the political utility of military power.

OPERATIONAL DOCTRINE

Soviet military doctrine is relatively simple in its aim, which is to win wars. The term "deterrence," in regard to military power, is seen differently in the East than in the West. In the West, which has essentially accepted Brodie's 1946 view, the purpose of having forces in being is to provide deterrence; thus, the contradiction of the Strategic Air Command's motto: "Peace is our profession." In the East, if deterrence flows from military readiness, well and good, but that is the business of the political leadership. "No Soviet military officer would be assigned 'deterrence' as his primary mission. His task is to be able to fight and win."[7] Therefore, once a political decision is made to use force, the Soviet military view would be to prevail; it would not be to achieve limited aims but to crush the adversary. There is no Soviet doctrine of "limited war" as such.

According to Soviet military doctrine, the ideal war in Europe is a single campaign blitzkrieg that is won quickly. The longer war continues, the higher the risk to the Soviets that the West will use nuclear weapons or that other military or political factors will spin out of control. "According to the Russian way of thinking, if it came to a long war the Soviet Union would almost certainly lose," which is not an unnatural reaction for a military doctrine that believes in "winners" and "losers."[8] Losing in the Kremlin's eyes might take several forms. A catastrophic nuclear exchange would destroy the social fabric of communism and, incidentally, the Soviet leadership. A long war would allow the economic might of the West to overwhelm the USSR and, because of the strains imposed on the Soviet empire, would erode the USSR's control of events. Soviet military planning, therefore, is oriented toward a quick win, either with nuclear weapons or without them.

From Clausewitz and other strategists, Lenin and his followers have drawn military lessons that emphasize mass, speed, and surprise.[9] Being good students the Soviet General Staff over the years have evolved a doctrine of theater war that is wholly offensive in its operational orientation.[10] This conviction that only offensive action can bring decisive results also has been reflected in shaping the composition and size of the armed forces, notably in the tank-oriented organization of the ground forces and their relative paucity of support and logistic units. There is little force-strategy mismatch in the Soviet military establishment. On the theater level, today's Soviet army operates with what Nathan Leites calls a certain style of war.[11]

THE SHATTERING BLOW

The most notable feature of the style is the belief in using maximum force. It is especially urgent that the first blow be delivered with shattering force at the critical point. One Soviet military writer of the 1920s has noted:

> 'Earlier,' Tukhachevskii observed already in the 1930s, 'one began by defeating the secondary forces of the adversary, and finished . . . with his definitive crushing. Now one begins . . . with a basic decisive strike and defers until later the . . . defeat of the weaker echeloned units of the enemy.'[12]

Dealing the shattering blow must be accomplished by massed forces, combining all means of firepower even under the risk of nuclear counterattack. It becomes essential to subject the enemy to a virtual storm of fire to prevent him from recovering the ability to resist. Thus there must be no letup; the tempo of the attack must be maintained without relief, around the clock, and until the enemy is decisively defeated.

SPEED

Emphasis on speed is a hallmark of Soviet offensive doctrine. Rapidity of attack gains surprise, reduces the enemy's ability to respond, and takes from the enemy time he would use against Soviet forces. Soviet manuals therefore stress meeting engagements, rapid reaction to unforeseen conditions, and speed of decision.

Whether this actually can be carried out in practice is questionable. All of Soviet society discourages initiative and risk-taking. Suvorov's account of life as a company grade officer does not show a service that encourages initiative, in the Western sense, among lower echelons of command. Von Mellenthin points out that the Soviet definition of initiative refers to acting in the best interests of the unit as a whole rather than acting independently. "The capacity for independent action within the broad framework of missions is neither alive nor welcome," he writes; "Soviet military leadership insists on 'leading all troop units without interruption, and at all times organizing their combat actions and exerting *uninterrupted control.*' "[13] The U.S. Army's doctrine teaches that planning rigidity is a weak point that can be exploited in Soviet operational doctrine.

It should be noted, though, that if one's doctrine is wedded to mass and incessant attack, and one has the commensurate resources, then rigidity and highly centralized control make sense. If Soviet rigidity means single-minded concentration on an objective, then the weak point might not be so weak, even if battlefield leaders are allowed only a small degree of flexibility by Western standards.

There is more to centralized control, however, than just selection of objectives. There are the thousands of decisions that have to be made on the fringe of battle, such as choosing routes, timing marches, and planning for logistic supply of myriad essential materiels. Competent staffs can do the required plug-and-chug routine planning, but many critical decisions have to be made in the process. In a highly centralized system, a great deal of buck-passing message traffic and reliance on guidance from higher headquarters would be the rule. Here, as much as on the battlefield, may be the true weakness of a centralized command system.

To move these large numbers of units toward the battlefield in a dispersed but operationally useful manner, the Soviets have adopted a doctrine of echeloning their forces at all levels so that every formation from company upward moves in at least two echelons (see Diagram 1). The company deploys for combat in a first and second echelon, being itself part of the battalion's first or second echelon, the battalion part of the regiment, and the regiment part of the division. In an

Diagram 1. Breakthrough Attack Deployments (Tank Units): Soviet Echelonment Concept

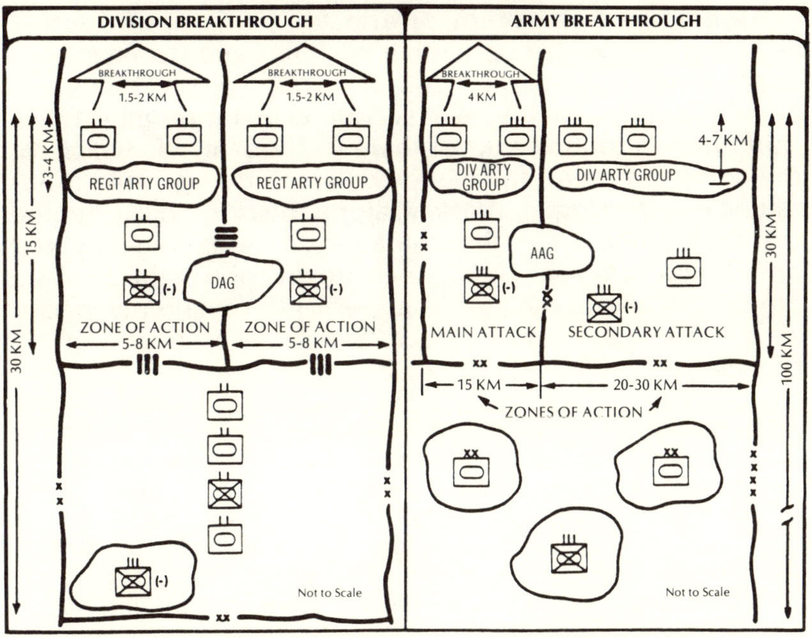

Source: Department of the Army, *FM 71-2: The Tank and Mechanized Infantry Battalion Task Force* (Washington, DC: Government Printing Office, 1977), p. 5–12.

attack, as one battalion, or regiment, or division is ground down, it is withdrawn whole from the battle or held in place and another fresh formation passes through and takes over. A policy of this nature is designed specifically for the offensive, as units being relieved can in effect stand still, and replacement units can simply attack through them and continue to press the enemy. Seen from the front, the effect of these successive echelons would be like waves crashing onto a beach, one after the other, preceded by a rolling storm of artillery fire and possibly chemical attack supported by armed helicopters and close support aircraft.

A word of caution should be injected about the echelonment doctrine. Soviet analyses are quite clear that when the structure of the enemy's defense alters so should the structure of the attacking force. The Soviets are not always committed to attacking irrevocably in echelons, nor is the distinction between echelons, in terms of actual dispositions on the ground, easy to discern.

In addition to a constant supply of fresh units for the battlefield, echelonment of attacking forces in depth is intended to provide operational flexibility and strong mass. A Western military analyst, Colonel (ret.) Trevor Dupuy, has pointed out that the use of a second echelon permits a rapid shift of effort to the flanks or to new axes of attack, which was the concept behind the Napoleonic column as well.[14] Thus, as first echelon forces attack all along the front, opportunities that are opened by the first combats can be exploited by fresh units in follow-on echelons which are diverted in their forward movement toward the promising sectors. From his perspective as a Soviet regimental officer, Suvorov has described the process:

> Soviet tactics are of the utmost simplicity; they can be condensed into a single phrase—the maximum concentration of forces in the decisive sector . . . at Kursk in 1943 . . . during an offensive by nine forward battalions only one managed to break any ground. Immediately, the commander of the regiment to which the battalion belonged concentrated all his resources at that point, on a front one kilometer wide. His divisional commander thereupon threw all his forces into this sector. The breach became wider and deeper and within half an hour the corps commander's reserves began to arrive. Within three

hours, 27 of the 36 battalions belonging to the corps had been brought in to fight in the narrow sector, which was by now 7 kilometers wide . . . as soon as he was informed of the breakthrough, the Commander of the Central Front . . . rushed an entire Army to the spot, with an Air Army to cover the operations. A few days later the Supreme Commander added his own reserve Army to the forces.[15]

This kind of "expanding torrent" is the basic Soviet maneuver concept today. Recently, however, there have been two additional developments in the Soviets' operations which also must be considered as significant adjuncts to their basic doctrine. The first is a developing operational concept pertaining to formations called operational maneuver groups (OMG).[16] Although the outlines of this development are still not settled to Western analysts, the thought is to form highly mobile armored formations to punch through Western defenses and attack objectives deep in NATO's rear, especially tactical nuclear weapons and command and control headquarters. The OMGs would be division size, or larger, and would be employed by the army commander, the Soviet Field Army being roughly equivalent to the U.S. corps level. Each OMG would contain armored and motorized rifle units mounted in armored fighting vehicles, self-propelled artillery, and dedicated air support by both armed helicopter units and fixed-wing fighter and close support aircraft. An OMG, as it is presently understood, would not be a special formation but one constituted for the occasion by the army commander, perhaps from an echelon of an advancing army, and task-organized for a specific mission.

The emergence of the OMG concept is the result of the Soviets' close analyses of NATO's defensive strengths and weaknesses, and illustrates their willingness to learn from experience.[17] The Soviets had extensive World War II experience with fast-moving task forces similar to OMGs. When their offensives began encountering German defenses layered in depth, for example, mobile groups were formed around Red tank armies to exploit opportunities to breach forward defenses and quickly enter the Germans' rear before the gaps could be plugged. Therefore, a defender's lack of a strong mobile reserve encourages the formation and use of OMGs. The historical analogy familiar to many Western readers would be General Heinz Guderian's armored corps' operations in central France once the 1st Panzer Division had crossed the Meuse in 1940.

Soviet operational helicopter doctrine is the second development that must be closely watched by NATO planners. The USSR has long considered and planned for the use of vertical envelopment. During the Second World War the Soviets conducted numerous parachute operations against German rear areas, and current operational doctrine calls for the use of conventional parachute troops and special forces to seize critical objectives, disrupt movement, and conduct espionage operations deep in the rear. Toward this end, the Soviets maintain seven airborne divisions and a number of elite special purpose *Spetznaz* units that are trained to conduct raids and sabotage. They also have added to their ranks about eight air assault brigades, composed of three rifle battalions each, plus support troops. Apparently they are learning about the tactical utility of helicopters in Afghanistan just as the United States did in Vietnam. A recent reorganization has assigned a helicopter regiment of about 400 aircraft to each army, at least in East Germany and to forces along the border with China; about one-half are supposed to be Mi-24 gunships, which also carry troops.[18]

The sum of these changes in operational doctrine is a greatly enhanced Soviet threat to NATO's rear, practically a Russian version of Deep Attack except with operationally mobile ground forces rather than air power. This operational maneuver concept must be worrisome to NATO planners and must lead to increased Western attention to rear-area security, among other things. If the Soviets continue to attach paramount importance to a quick victory before NATO can use its nuclear weapons, then Western planners must expect that Soviet conventional doctrine and forces in the remaining decades of this century will continue to emphasize massed tank and mechanized forces attacking in great numbers supported by powerful fires and attempts at deep strategic and operational penetration. These maneuvers will be carried out by specialized formations simultaneously attacking deep into NATO's rear to destroy tactical nuclear assets, isolate command facilities, and paralyze NATO maneuver forces. If Soviet force structure continues to follow doctrine, as it probably will, then tank and mechanized forces will continue modernization and more specialized formations, notably air-portable ones, will be formed. Whether the Soviets' resulting structures can be trained adequately in the kinds of complex and risky operations their doctrine envisions is another question. Such operations call for imagination and relative freedom of action on the part of junior leaders.

SURPRISE

Surprise is a principle of war highly favored by the Soviets and their allies, and evidence of their appreciation of catching the enemy unaware shows in their writings, training, and in the actual execution of their most recent military operations in Czechoslovakia and Afghanistan, where their successes in achieving strategic surprise reflect a growing sophistication in deception operations.[19]

Surprise in wartime can be achieved on strategic, operational, and tactical levels. Tactical surprise is highly sought on the battlefield, where the classic military arts of deception, camouflage, and cover are used to keep the immediate enemy off balance and guessing where and when the attack will come and at what strength. The history of war is filled with examples of successful tactical surprise; the ambush and the unexpected rush at dawn frequently can lead to greater success if the attacker is bold enough and has prepared in advance to exploit his advantage. Tactical surprise is usually a prerequisite for operational surprise. The German Ardennes counteroffensive in the winter of 1944 began with this idea and achieved operational level success because the Germans exploited their tactical breakthrough. It failed because the Reich ultimately could not sustain the attack or reverse the Allied strategic advantage in manpower and materiel.

Strategic surprise is harder to achieve but may have decisive results. If strategic surprise also achieves tactical and operational surprise—that is, surprise is gained on all three levels and is backed with sufficient means—the enemy may be knocked from the war with a single stroke. Since weapons are more mobile and have greater effect now than in the nineteenth century, the idea of a single stroke war, or a war of one campaign, is sufficiently tempting that surprise attack has become the preferred method for starting conventional wars in the twentieth century. The German assault on Russia, the Japanese attack on Pearl Harbor, the Israeli preemptive attacks of 1967, the Warsaw Pact's rapid invasion of Czechoslovakia in 1968, and the Soviet occupation of Kabul in 1980 were all strategic surprises aimed at quickly overthrowing the opposition; in some cases they succeeded. In the U.S. short war doctrine, there is an echo of tacit acceptance of the Soviet war of one campaign, which NATO hopes to terminate either by defending a Pact attack on the IGB, negotiating, or resorting to nuclear weapons. No nation intentionally starts a protracted conflict, and some of the longest and bloodiest were begun as short wars. But there is a difference, and a crucial one, between a potential attacker planning a short war and a defender planning one.

Even with the advent of space surveillance and instant communications, hoodwinking one's opponent on the strategic level is still possible. The reason is that, while armies may be moved about and warlike preparations made, the key to achieving strategic surprise is concealing intentions from the proposed victim, not necessarily preparations. In every case mentioned above, there was some indication of impending attack. While tactical intentions were not clear, the U.S. government knew in December 1941 that war with Japan was probable. Likewise, Stalin knew that Hitler was going to attack him eventually, but he misjudged the Nazis' timing and disregarded the warnings of his frontline commanders to whom it was obvious the Germans were preparing to attack. The Germans rolled up the British and French armies in the summer of 1940 by achieving strategic and operational surprise. In their turn at deception and feints, the Allies were able to conceal from Hitler the location and time of their invasion of France in 1944 with such success that, even after the assault had begun, the German High Command was not convinced it was the main attack.

At what the West would refer to as the strategic level, the Soviets acknowledge the difficulty of achieving true surprise. In his study of Soviet blitzkrieg theory, P. H. Vigor has noted:

> Tactical surprise has often been achieved; strategic surprise, seldom. This is because the number of troops

required for strategic operations is so enormous that it is virtually impossible to conceal their presence from the enemy. Strategic surprise has consequently only been attainable when the purpose for which the troops have been assembled has been managed to be disguised, and the intended enemy lulled into false security.[20]

To the Soviets, therefore, strategic surprise is achievable by concealing intentions or the scale of a buildup, not by concealing forces as such. The institution of long-term mobilization exercises, even without a specific intent to attack now or in the future, might serve a strategic offensive purpose by offering a standby cloak under which emergency mobilization could take place if required; this might serve to achieve strategic surprise. One writer has postulated a number of strategic deception measures that would not conceal the fact of mobilization but only its ultimate intent, thus leaving Western analysts to count divisions and guess at intentions.[21]

In his study of Soviet strategy, Vigor has derived four principles of the Soviets' theory of surprise attack which illustrate their military thought at all levels: strategic, operational, and tactical. Surprise may be achieved first by the *place of attack*—that is, using deception and camouflage to move troops and attacking in locations where, because of difficult terrain, the enemy would be unsuspecting. Second is the *date of the attack*; in other words, attacking at a time of year that would be unfavorable and thereby unexpected. Vigor uses as an example the timing of Soviet invasions with periods when Western officials are on vacation or holiday. Third, the *time of the attack* is also vital, darkness being preferred in spite of the difficulties that this poses for the Soviets' own troops, and at times they seem to avoid the hourly and half-hourly "hacks" preferred in U.S. exercises. Finally, *new weapons and methods* may enhance surprise. Vigor points out that the Soviet Union tends to use unexpected operational methods to catch its enemies off balance; for example, employing lower-grade forces for the Czechoslovak invasion in 1968 when most Western analysts were watching the Soviets' more elite units for indications of their intentions.

According to Vigor, at least one Soviet theoretician believes that counterelectronic warfare is a separate method of securing surprise. Western doctrine would consider that to be a part of the overall deception operations to complement the efforts above.[22]

ORGANIZATION

The Soviet armed forces consist of five branches: the Strategic Rocket Forces, Ground Forces (army), National Air Defense Troops (Voyska PVO), air forces, and navy.[23] Military service in the Soviet Union is compulsory for all males, and a term of service is two years in the army and air force, and two to three years in the navy and border guards. Total personnel in the Soviet armed forces is about 5,050,000, not counting border guards, internal security troops, and some engineer and construction units. Unlike the U.S. armed forces, the Soviet armed forces are headed by a General Staff which unifies direction of the military services and reports to the Main Military Council of the Defense Ministry, headed by its commissar of defense. The closest functional equivalent to the Soviet General Staff is the pre-World War I German army General Staff.[24]

A recent reorganization of Soviet forces has established three theaters: Western, Southern, and Far Eastern, with a Central Reserve area in the USSR itself. The Western theater is then subdivided into theaters of military operations (TVD).[25] Soviet Ground Forces and Frontal Aviation are further assigned to sixteen military districts within the Soviet Union. Upon mobilization, these districts become fronts, which typically contain 3 or 4 Combined Arms Armies of about 5 divisions, 1 tank army (4 to 5 divisions), 1 tactical air army, and support and are subordinated to a TVD or a theater (see Map 3).

There are four Soviet force groups outside the USSR's frontiers, the most important being the Group of Soviet Forces, Germany (GSFG), headquartered near Berlin; the three additional ones are the Northern Group (Poland), Central Group (Czechoslovakia), and Southern Group (Hungary). Thus Soviet Ground Forces are generally organized in peacetime under the headquarters that would command them in war, a departure from U.S. units in the United States but true of most NATO forces in West Germany.

Soviet Ground Forces number 1,800,000, of which about 1,400,000 are conscripts; the Soviet forces do not have a large

Map 3. Soviet Theaters

Source: North Atlantic Treaty Organization, *NATO and the Warsaw Pact: Force Comparisons* (Brussels, 1984), p. 52. Reprinted by permission.

permanent noncommissioned corps as is normally found in Western armies. Soviet Ground Forces eschew the varieties of organizations found in the West as well. Most Soviet and Warsaw Pact forces are organized into fairly standard tank divisions and motorized rifle divisions, with some airborne and air assault troops.

The Soviet army consists of 50 tank divisions and 134 motorized rifle divisions, 7 airborne divisions, 8 new air assault brigades, 15 artillery divisions, and numerous independent tank regiments, engineer regiments, and other support forces. Soviet divisions are smaller than their U.S. counterparts. Firepower is about the same, but Soviet forces are organized with less logistic and maintenance support, which reflects their emphasis on a fast campaign and a short war in which supply and repair services are less critical. For example, in a motorized rifle regiment, maintenance, first aid, and other service troops make up only about 10 percent of the total regimental strength.[26]

The numbers of Soviet divisions are rendered somewhat less formidable when the manning system used to maintain so large an army is understood. The USSR keeps ground units at three levels of readiness: Category 1, with complete equipment and from 75 to 100 percent of strength; Category 2, with units complete in fighting vehicles but with only 50 to 75 percent strength in manpower; and Category 3, with fighting vehicles possibly complete but older models and manpower maintained at below 50 percent strength, although the percentage may be changing slightly. This breakdown makes mobilization policies extremely important when considering both Pact and NATO employment strategy.[27]

Soviet air forces also have undergone a reorganization. Although the details are not completely clear, there are now 20 regional commands of varying strengths of fighter-attack aircraft and 5 air armies of long- and medium-range bombers. The rationale behind the regional command reorganization is apparently to bring the air forces more closely under control of the TVDs. This is particularly interesting in terms of enhancing the coordination of air and ground forces in fast-moving situations that demand quick operational response. Soviet air force units in the 20 air commands number 5,950 combat aircraft and 2,300 combat helicopters. It should be noted that a new ground-attack aircraft, the Su-25, has come into production, a fact that indicates that the Soviets are learning the value of close air support in Afghanistan.

The growth of the Soviet navy has been one of the most interesting strategic developments in the postwar period. Russian naval tradition never has been particularly strong, being generally most concerned with the control of the Baltic and Black seas. As the czars completed their territorial expansion in the nineteenth century, however, Russia's competitors increasingly were maritime powers. In the Crimean War and other operations in the eastern Mediterranean, Britain successfully opposed Russian interests with sea power. The focus of Sir Halford Mackinder's heartland versus maritime thesis, and Nicholas Spykman's subsequent amplification, dealt with this historic collision between an expanding continental power and the rimland states.[28]

To a certain extent the Soviet navy is an adjunct of the Ground Forces. Although the Communist leadership from the 1920s has taken some interest in the USSR's maritime defense, Soviet doctrine continues to emphasize the primacy of land operations, which is natural considering the Soviet Union's geography, history, and the domination of its joint and combined commands by tank officers.[29] An exception is the Soviet nuclear-powered ballistic missile submarine (SSBN) fleet, which occupies a special place in Kremlin strategic planning, like the American SSBN force in the U.S. Navy. The Soviet navy's strategic function appears to have been the subject of Kremlin debate for some time. The present chief of the navy, Admiral S. G. Gorshkov, makes an argument in *The Sea Power of the State* for all the classic advantages for gaining command of the sea and argues for a broader understanding of the uses to carry out a proper naval strategy.

> Unlike the past, when the main armed force of imperialism was made up of land armies, in the present-day conditions one of the principal roles in the armed struggle against the countries of socialism is assigned to naval forces. However, bearing in mind the experience of history, *demonstrating the total untenability of military doctrines oriented to the use of one branch of the armed forces or one kind of weapon,* the imperialists contemplate the development of ground, air and also missile forces while at the same time laying the main stress on missile forces.[30]

Although to a Westerner he sounds like any service chief making a pitch for his budget, Gorshkov appears to have had some success. The concept of sea power is apparently being taken seriously by Soviet leaders, and sufficient resources are being allocated to the admiral to give him an even more impressive blue-water navy, already the world's largest, including eventually conventional aircraft carriers. Only time will tell if the Soviet Union will truly remain a maritime power, or if Gorshkov is playing Colbert to the Kremlin's Louis XIV.

One naval analyst has derived five doctrinal Soviet naval missions in wartime, although their priority is not settled:

strikes against the shores by submarine-launched missiles, destruction of enemy naval forces, interdiction of enemy sea lines of communication (SLOC), direct support of ground force operations, and protection of one's own SLOCs.[31] Although there is no equivalent of the U.S. naval doctrine of air strikes against land targets, or power projection from carrier decks, the construction of Soviet conventional aircraft carriers might portend a doctrinal change in coming years.

The mission of protecting one's own SLOCs is significant. Historically the Soviet Union, a heartland power, has not been dependent on SLOCs, except possibly in the Baltic or the Gulf of Finland where there might be an effort to circumvent dependence on unruly or doubtful allies.[32] If the Soviet navy is beginning to consider this as a mission, then the inference is that the fleet would be defending routes to allies outside the continental USSR, or to Soviet overseas bases. The Soviet conventional aircraft carrier under construction in 1984 on the Black Sea is obviously a major investment in power-projection forces.[33] Other elements of a Western-style carrier strike force, escorts, attack submarines, and replenishment ships are already in place. The move toward aircraft carrier-based naval striking forces, if in fact the Soviets are doing so, points to a sea control doctrine rooted in classic geopolitical thought, and imperialistic thought at that, rather than in the more familiar Soviet-Marxist strategies to defend the revolution—and the USSR—and to support indigenous revolutions. The significance of the mission of interdicting the enemy's SLOCs has a special importance in regard to NATO.

The major Soviet fleets must operate from bases that, with the possible exception of those in the Pacific, are vulnerable to blockade and interdiction. This vulnerability would make it likely that, in preparation for war, or at the onset of hostilities, the fleets would "flush" toward their operational areas, a strategic warning signal of the first magnitude. The submarine fleet especially can be expected to begin early movement, in particular the SSBNs in port.

The Northern Fleet, based in the Barents Sea at the top of the Scandinavian peninsula at Severomorsk, is the largest of the Soviet fleet concentrations. In war these fleet elements would probably attempt to enter North Atlantic operational areas via routes past Greenland, Iceland, or the United Kingdom. Here are based 181 Soviet submarines, including 46

SSBNs, 196 surface combatants, and numerous supporting craft.

The Baltic Fleet is headquartered at Baltiysk in the Gulf of Danzig and well down the Baltic toward its exits, although units of the fleet are distributed along the coast as far north as Kronstadt. If the fleet's wartime mission should require it to break out into the Atlantic, it would have to force the hazardous waters of the Kattegat and Skagerrak between Denmark, Sweden, and Norway; this is not a happy prospect for the Soviets. The Baltic Fleet disposes of 30 submarines and 325 surface combatants of all sizes.

The Black Sea Fleet has the disadvantage of having to pass the Bosporus to enter the Mediterranean Sea. Based on Sevastopol, the fleet consists of 25 submarines and 272 surface combatants, including 2 of the Soviet Union's 3 *Kiev* class 37,000-ton VSTOL aircraft carriers.[34] The fleet maintains a forward-deployed squadron in the Mediterranean, generally consisting of about 12 surface combatants, 2 amphibious transports, and various auxiliary vessels.

The Pacific Fleet, based at Vladivostok, maintains Soviet naval elements throughout the Pacific and Indian oceans at bases in Vietnam, South Yemen, and Ethiopia. The fleet has 120 submarines, including 28 SSBNs; 314 surface combat ships, including the third *Kiev* VSTOL carrier; 20 amphibious transports; a large number of major auxiliary ships, derived by the need to support such a widespread fleet; and the largest of the naval aviation contingents, with a total of about 330 combat aircraft, including 120 long-range bombers.

THE WARSAW PACT

The origins of the Warsaw Pact lie in Stalin's determination to erect a postwar security, or buffer, zone for the Soviet Union in Eastern Europe, continuing a tradition of Russian domination that has been the case more often than not in the history of the region. Andrzej Korbonski has listed four major objectives behind Stalin's move west: to deny the region to possible enemies, to ensure that whoever governed the region remained friendly to the USSR, to use the region's resources to aid Soviet economic recovery and development, and to use the region as a springboard for a possible attack on the West.[35]

How reliable the Pact is as an instrument of Soviet policy is a question not easily answered. Certainly the USSR, from the very beginning, has exercised tight control over the Pact. When the treaty was signed in 1955 the Eastern bloc armed forces had just been purged and reorganized by the Soviets, whose military advisers were prominent throughout the region and exercised command in the armies of East European countries. A Soviet general officer, Konstantin Rokossovskiy, was then defense minister of Poland. The world was treated to the sight of a Soviet general signing a treaty with his own state. East European armies were required to be armed with Soviet weapons, use Soviet doctrine, and accept Soviet advisers and commanders in high-level positions.

In spite of such Soviet domination, however, the Pact is not without its strains. The most obvious splits have been East Germany in 1953, Hungary in 1956, Czechoslovakia in 1968, Poland in 1981, and the withdrawal of Albania from the Pact in 1968. Romania has shown an aversion to participating in Pact exercises. There are reports that the USSR has tried to interest its allies in deploying regular units outside Europe, particularly to Vietnam, along the Sino-Soviet border, and in Afghanistan, but has been rebuffed.

The question of reliability probably turns on the circumstances of the war that the East Europeans would be expected to fight. Most analysts agree that the East European armed forces would fight well in defense of their own soil. Their utility in an aggressive attack on the West, however, is questionable. Aside from their traditional dislike for their Soviet ally, the mood in Eastern Europe in 1985 is strongly toward distancing itself from Soviet military initiatives and increasing economic and political contact with its Western cousins.[36] Non-Soviet Pact military spending lags far behind the USSR's expenditures.[37] If the Soviet Union's leadership were to decide on aggression against the West, one of the frictions against which it would have to contend would be its own allies. While the Soviets would probably be able to coerce the leaders of East Germany, Poland, Czechoslovakia, Hungary, and other Pact countries, the process of doing so would certainly run grave risks of compromising surprise at strategic, operational, and tactical levels. For a Soviet war planner, Eastern Europe is a doubtful ally.

Would the Pact fight however war came? Much would depend on early success and speed. If the Pact members were convinced that a preemptive attack was necessary to defend their own soil, and if it went well, and quickly, they would probably persist. But, if the attack stalled and the Soviets began to suffer reverses, then East European support might well fade. There are ethnic questions also. The East Germans are the best trained and most reliable of the East European armies, but their probable employment would pit them against their own relatives in West Germany, thereby creating a chancy disposition. The Poles would probably fight West Germans—any Germans—but they have no traditional animosities toward the United States, France, or Britain. Indeed, next to the Germans, Poles dislike the Soviets most. Czechoslovak forces have been demoralized since 1968, and their utility is questionable under any circumstances; likewise, the Hungarians. Neither does Romania appear to be a particularly enthusiastic member of the Pact. Only Bulgaria, with its traditional pro-Soviet outlook, offers anything close to the kind of reliability that the Soviets would look for before embarking on a major war in Europe[38] (see Table 3).

The four Pact countries whose forces in Eastern Europe immediately threaten the central front—the USSR, Czechoslovakia, East Germany, and Poland—together maintain 50

Table 3. East European Reliability in a Warsaw Pact Attack on NATO

	Short-Term Operation		Long-Term Operation	
	Successful Operation	Unsuccessful Operation	Successful Operation	Unsuccessful Operation
Poland	Medium low	Very low	Medium low	Very low
East Germany	Medium	Low	Medium	Very low
Czechoslovakia	Very low	Very low	Very low	Very low
Hungary	Very low	Very low	Very low	Very low
Romania	Very low	Very low	Very low	Very low
Bulgaria	Medium	Low	Medium	Low

Source: Dale A. Herspring and Ivan Volgyes, "Political Reliability in the Eastern European Warsaw Pact Armies," *Armed Forces and Society* 6, no. 3 (Winter 1980): 289. Reprinted by permission of Seven Locks Press.

Category 1 armored and mechanized divisions; over one-third (20) are non-Soviet Pact divisions (see Table 4). While the number and proportion of Soviet units to Pact units could be increased by exercises, covert mobilization, and movement or other means of deception, some or all Pact forces would clearly have a frontline role in a Soviet western offensive, and their value increases in scenarios involving limited mobilization. As in Western Europe and the USSR, the frontline Pact states have large reservoirs of trained manpower and numerous home-guard organizations that would only indirectly affect the opening stages of a war with NATO.

CONCLUSIONS

Any assessment of the military balance between the Warsaw Pact and NATO, based on manpower and hardware comparisons, must contain a large measure of subjectivity. Even informed subjective judgment is clouded in masses of data on the Western side and on the Eastern by the veil of secrecy that the Soviets attach to even the most mundane military issues. The veil can be lifted, however fleetingly, and what is seen can be analyzed.

There is no doubt that the armed forces of the Soviet Union are large and very strong, perhaps the most powerful ever assembled by any nation in peacetime. Certainly they

Table 4. The Non-Soviet Central Front Powers

Country	Category 1	Category 2	Category 3	Aircraft
Czechoslovakia	6	—	4	471
East Germany	6	—	—	359
Poland	8	2	3	140
TOTAL	20	2	7	970

Sources: *Military Balance, 1983–1984*, pp. 14–24; and William Kaufmann, "Nuclear Deterrence in Central Europe," in John D. Steinbruner and Leon V. Segal, eds., *Alliance Security: NATO and the No-First-Use Question* (Washington, DC: Brookings Institution, 1983), p. 57. Reprinted by permission of Brookings Institution.

Note: Evidently 1 Czech tank division between 1982 and 1984 slipped from Category 1 to Category 2.

seem to be more powerful than required simply for security of the Soviet state. Furthermore, these forces are directed by political intentions openly and consistently hostile to the West. The dynamics of its political doctrine, and a genuine historical apprehension of hostile neighbors, has made, and is making, the USSR the twentieth-century equivalent of Prussia, the "army with a country." In the Soviet Union, however, the political leadership remains firmly in charge. The unity of effort thus achieved between the Soviet military leadership and the political masters of the Kremlin has allowed the Soviet army a continuity between grand strategy, doctrine, force structure, and tactics that should be the envy of Western military professionals. In the USSR the study of war receives an emphasis unknown in the United States or Western Europe. Soviet military leaders study their business thoroughly and, as a rule, their professional schools are longer and more demanding than comparable NATO ones.[39]

Soviet equipment is good. The technological lead that the United States confidently held a decade ago has significantly narrowed, and in some fields may soon disappear completely. As expected in a military philosophy that stresses mass and speed, Soviet equipment is rugged, relatively immune to mishandling, generally reliable, and there is much of it. The Soviets stockpile older items of equipment and then pass these on to their allies, leaving the USSR with enormous stocks of war materiel with which to form new divisions should the necessity arise.

Soviet manpower is also more than adequate, and the wartime performance of the Red Army from 1941 to 1945 testifies to the bravery and hardihood of the Russian common soldier and to the resolution of his officers. Standards of discipline in the Soviet army today, at least to most outward appearances, indicate that the forces would be able to stand fire and perform in battle. On closer examination, however, some contradictions begin to arise when objective Soviet doctrine, tactics, and force structure are cast against leadership, management, and military style, subjective factors having as much to do with the nature and history of Soviet politics as with military training.

The traditional Soviet dependence on mass, which grew from the hordes of peasants employed by the czars and perpetuated itself—unavoidably and successfully—in World

War II, seems inappropriate for any lightning attack against NATO. The huge tonnages required, the strains on roads and rail, and the demand for secrecy in the USSR and among the Poles or East Germans argues for smaller armies if the present doctrine of "preventive attack" is to be followed.

There are signs that this difficulty has been recognized, and that the Soviet army is planning its OMG and air-portable operations, with an eye toward increasing the speed with which it can cut through opposition, paralyze resistance, and strike deep into the vital rear. Unfortunately for the Soviets their history and society discourage the type of independent, risk-taking leadership that can execute these most difficult maneuvers. To do the kinds of things they plan, a virtual revolution in Soviet military practice is necessary. They would be required to retrain their system from one that stresses constant control of every detail to one that emphasizes mission-type orders, trust, and low-level initiative. But, if the Soviets continue to persist and their doctrine continues to change, a gap, which exists today, widens between what they *plan* to do and what they actually *can* do. They have read Clausewitz too literally; their doctrine begins to reflect what a German army could do but not a Russian one.

As mentioned previously, this point can be overstated. The Soviets became better at independent operations and showed more tactical flexibility in the late stages of World War II. Furthermore, massed tanks employed against a weak point can moot doctrinal faults. But, as the skill of the opposition increases, the aggressor's margin for error shrinks. Although NATO is outgunned overall, the balance today remains sufficiently uncertain as to make a Soviet conventional attack against NATO a very risky undertaking. Worse still, from the Kremlin's point of view, should be that almost no matter how much the hardware improves, the offensive orientation that the Soviets have evolved will demand more and more freedom and Western-style initiative within their forces, which directly contradicts the present Soviet social environment.

Gaps do exist between theory and practice in every army, but there are other weaknesses. The unreliability of the Soviet Union's allies is a major complication, inhibiting its ability to strike with surprise but requiring a speedy decision before its position in Eastern Europe can unravel. Moreover, China menaces its eastern borders. When all these and other subjective factors are matched against the arsenals of tanks and planes, a picture emerges that makes possible a successful conventional defense by NATO, provided Western logistics and doctrine are up to the task.

Notes

[1] Steve F. Kime, "The Soviet View of War," *Comparative Strategy* 2, no. 3 (1980): 208.

[2] Marshal I. C. Bagramyan, "The USSR is Threatened from Many Directions," *Canadian Defence Quarterly* (Summer 1982): 6.

[3] Edward N. Luttwak, *The Grand Strategy of the Soviet Union* (New York: St. Martin's Press, 1983), p. 18.

[4] F. W. von Mellenthin, R. H. S. Stolfi, and E. Sobik, *NATO Under Attack* (Durham, NC: Duke University Press, 1984), p. 52.

[5] Viktor Suvorov, *Inside the Soviet Army* (New York: Macmillan, 1983), p. 245.

[6] Carl von Clausewitz, *On War* (Princeton, NJ: Princeton University Press, 1976), p. 119.

[7] Kime, "Soviet View of War," p. 211.

[8] P. H. Vigor, *Soviet Blitzkrieg Theory* (New York: St. Martin's Press, 1983), p. 2. Vigor makes an excellent presentation of an "ideal" Soviet surprise attack that, on reflection, highlights both the strategic futility and operational difficulty of such a course of action for the Soviets. For the Vigor model to succeed, there must be total surprise at all levels. Brodie acknowledged in 1946 that "in international politics today few things are more certain than that an attack must have an antecedent hostility of obviously grave character." (Brodie, *Absolute Weapon*, p. 74). That fact has not changed in the forty years since.

[9] V. Y. Savkin, *The Basic Principles of Operational Art and Tactics* (Moscow, 1972), trans. U.S. Air Force (Washington, DC: Government Printing Office), p. 22.

[10] Mako, *U.S. Ground Forces*, p. 40.

[11] Nathan Leites, "The Soviet Style of War," in Derek Leebart, ed., *Soviet Military Thinking* (Boston: George Allen & Unwin, 1981), p. 185.

[12] Ibid., p. 188.

[13] Von Mellenthin, *NATO Under Attack*, pp. 94, 96 (emphasis added).

[14] Trevor N. Dupuy, "The Soviet Second Echelon: Is This a Red Herring?" *Armed Forces Journal* 119, no. 12 (August 1982): 62.

[15] Suvorov, *Inside the Soviet Army*, p. 172.

[16] In Western military terminology, "operational" applies to a level of combat between tactics and strategy at roughly the NATO corps-field army level or the Pact army-front. See *Operations* (1982), p. 2–3.

[17] C. N. Donnelly, "The Soviet Operational Maneuver Group—A New Challenge for NATO," *International Defense Review* 15, no. 9 (September 1982): 1179.

[18] *Military Balance, 1983–1984*, p. 11.

[19] For example, see Pavel A. Chuvikov, "Factors Determining the Fate of Contemporary War," in Harriet Fast Scott and William F. Scott, eds., *The Soviet Art of War* (Boulder, CO: Westview Press, 1982), pp. 132–36; Savkin, *Basic Principles*; and Richard K. Betts, *Surprise Attack* (Washington, DC: Brookings Institution, 1982).

[20] Vigor, *Soviet Blitzkrieg*, p. 82.

[21] Betts, *Surprise Attack*, p. 203.

[22] Vigor, *Soviet Blitzkrieg*, pp. 157–66.

[23] Except where otherwise noted, the following data are drawn from Collins, "U.S. and Soviet Trends Compared," *Military Balance*, pp. 53–80; and *Military Balance, 1983–1984*, pp. 14–18. The conclusions are those of the author.

[24] A good reference on the German General Staff system is Dupuy, *A Genius for War*. On the surface the German and Russian General Staff systems are similar. The most striking difference is the extent of Soviet party control over the military. The USSR's political leadership is suspicious of its generals and is quick to remove one who shows signs of too much power, as happened to Marshal G. K. Zhukov and, more recently, N. V. Ogarkov, chief of the Soviet General Staff. The party evidently intends that strict control will inhibit the growth of an elitist military class.

[25] *Military Balance, 1983–1984*, p. 11.

[26] Department of the Army, *Soviet Army Operations* (Washington, DC: Assistant Chief of Staff for Intelligence, 1978), p. 2–11. Accurate unclassified data on Soviet tables of organization are difficult to obtain, and this manual carefully notes that "the accuracy of the information is perishable, and does not constitute a valid basis for order of battle analysis." It is suitable, however, for this kind of general analysis.

[27] Mobilization is discussed in more detail in Chapter Four. Agreement on how fast the Soviets can mobilize and move their Category 2 and 3 divisions is possibly the key to addressing effective conventional defense strategy. On a lower level of sensibility, perceptions of how quickly the Soviets can reinforce the western front tend to divide maritime strategists from continentalists. For example, Jeffrey Record takes the view that Soviet units below Category 1 take from 30 to 120 days to be combat effective. (Record, *Sizing Up the Soviet Army*, pp. 21–22). William Kaufmann, in "Nuclear Deterrence in Central Europe," in Steinbruner and Segal, *Alliance Security*, p. 60, believes that these units would reinforce more quickly. Longer Soviet mobilization would allow NATO more warning time and more time to reinforce, and thus is justification for relying more on reserve forces located in the United States (the maritime argument), while more rapid Soviet mobilization makes the case for strong regular forces stationed or prepositioned in Europe. The methodology for arriving at estimates is difficult, involving guesswork about Soviet intentions in a given scenario.

There are various ways to label Soviet divisional categories: Roman numerals, arabic, and letters. This study uses the arabic system, as does *Military Balance, 1983–1984* and most other generally available sources.

[28] Halford Mackinder, *The Geographical Pivot of History* (1904; reprint ed., London: Royal Geographic Society, 1951); and Nicholas J. Spykman, *The Geography of the Peace* (New York: Harcourt, Brace, 1944). Colin S. Gray's observations on the subject are valuable. See *The Geopolitics of the Nuclear Era* (New York: Crane, Russak, 1977), pp. 31–50.

[29] Michael McCguire, "Soviet Naval Doctrine and Strategy," in Leebart, *Soviet Military Thinking*, p. 128.

[30] S. G. Gorshkov, *The Sea Power of the State*, p. 283 (Russian edition copyrighted by Voyenizdat, 1976; translation copyrighted 1979 by Pergamon Press and reprinted by Naval Institute Press, Annapolis, MD). Author's emphasis.

[31] McCguire, "Soviet Naval Doctrine and Strategy," p. 147.

[32] There have been reports that the USSR is considering alternate supply lines along the Baltic coast in order to bypass Poland. (*Military Balance, 1983–1984*, p. 19). However, such lines are not liable to be adequate replacements for land routes.

[33] Department of Defense, *Soviet Military Power* (Washington, DC: Department of Defense, 1984), p. 64.

[34] A fourth *Kiev* is being built at this writing. *Military Balance, 1983–1984*, p. 12.

[35] Andrzej Korbonski, "The Warsaw Treaty After Twenty-Five Years: An Entangling Alliance or an Empty Shell?" in Robert W. Clawson and Lawrence S. Kaplan, eds., *The Warsaw Pact: Political Purpose and Military Means* (Wilmington, DE: Scholarly Resources, 1982), p. 5.

[36] Ibid., p. 11.

[37] See, for example, Robert English, "Eastern Europe's Doves," *Foreign Policy*, no. 56 (Fall 1984): 44–60; or any of a number of popular and scholarly articles about East European economic progress and independence from Moscow.

[38] Dale A. Herspring and Ivan Volgyes, "Political Reliability in the Eastern European Warsaw Pact Armies," *Armed Forces and Society* 6, no. 3 (Winter 1980): 289–90.

[39] Scott, *Soviet Art of War*, p. 3.

Chapter Four

Surprise and Mobilization

DETERMINING RISK

CONSTRUCTING A COHERENT DEFENSE POLICY, like any tactical problem or business deal, requires an idea of the opposition's probable courses of action. Once this has been done, they must be put in some kind of order, say from most likely to least, so that military strategies can be developed and the required instruments of strategy—ships, planes, and tanks—can be budgeted, produced, and melded into useful tools. There are infinite numbers of marginal variations to basic scenarios, but the essence of strategic analysis is to find and keep to the major issues, separate them from the background clutter of technological fads and misinformation, and create realistic visions of the probable future.

Analyses of strategies of deterrence begin to raise a curtain on a critical difference between deterrence applied to nuclear weapons versus deterrence by conventional ones. There are not likely to be winners and losers in a nuclear exchange; nuclear fighting doctrines deal only in marginal advantage after deterrence fails. Conventional forces, on the other hand, derive their deterrent authority from the possibility that one side or the other may win. This, however, is uncomfortably close to the way the Soviets have continued to look at the purpose of military forces since the end of World War II. If the West reviews its concept of conventional defense, as it should, then the concept of deterrence itself may have to be overhauled to resemble, in its nonnuclear aspects, the Soviet model. The implications of this kind of doctrinal shift would be to continue nuclear deterrence but to embark on a conventional defense that rested on nonnuclear traditional strategy, doctrine, and even military objectives that would be compatible with "winning" a nonnuclear conflict in which nuclear use would be an ever present possibility.

Discussions of war in Europe should deal not only with conventional versus nuclear war but also with different gradations of conventional attack. Indeed, in an operational analysis of NATO-Pact strategies, the most important threshold is not between nuclear and nonnuclear attack but between reinforced and unreinforced attack by the Warsaw Pact.[1] In other words, one scenario is the "bolt-from-the-blue" attack from a standing start by the Warsaw Pact; the second is a partial mobilization of both sides, with the West lagging behind the Soviets and their allies.[2] A Western nonnuclear defense policy and supporting strategy, designed first to deter and then to defeat each of these possible scenarios, must be considered in terms of risk and consequence. Doing that requires understanding the Soviet viewpoint and policy concerning two essentials for fighting conventional war in Europe: surprise and mobilization.

There is a fundamental strategic asymmetry between West and East since NATO forces, meaning not only the forces themselves but also their logistic bases and command and control systems, are defensively deployed, and those of the Warsaw Pact and the Soviet Union, in particular, are designed for offensive operations from the outset. For the Soviets, an offensive military posture does not contradict their professed nonaggressive intent. It is objectively consistent with their military doctrine. If war becomes avoidable, the Soviet armed forces will react defensively in a militarily correct way by preemptively launching massed armored forces to breach NATO defenses and then by striking deeply into NATO's rear to split and fragment the Alliance, neutralize the Federal Republic, and drive the United States from the European continent.

TWO ASSUMPTIONS

Two general assumptions should be kept in mind. First, always assuming that the Soviets have decided that the risk of initiating nuclear war is disadvantageous to them, both sides at the beginning of hostilities will immediately mount intense campaigns to find and destroy the other's theater and tactical nuclear weapons. The Soviets will use air attacks against known storage and dispersion sites, raids by airborne troops, and fifth-column sabotage. This intense nuclear hide-and-seek system will continue as long as hostilities go on; no other targets will have as high a priority for both sides. In the destruction of nuclear weapons and their delivery systems, each side will seek to gain a decisive advantage in the tactical or theater nuclear balance and to prevent the opposition from doing likewise. A lopsided gain, by either a sudden change in the nuclear correlation or in the operational situation on the battlefield, could trigger nuclear use. Therefore, on both sides the estimated balance would be a constant input into planning estimates.

Second, since neither the East nor West would know in advance the duration of the conflict, each would continue mobilizing as if for a long war. As long as the nuclear balance remains questionable, and the actual survival of the nuclear powers is not immediately at risk, the prudent course of action for each side is to rely on conventional military operations to seek negotiating advantages that would lead to war termination on favorable terms. The validity of such a comfortable prewar assumption is questionable since, as fighting continues, purposes tend to change.[3] But the whole rationale of conventional defense is to avoid defeat and to emerge from the initial defensive stage in a posture to dominate the war conventionally for whatever objectives at that time seem correct to the political leadership.

MOBILIZATION

If the Soviets intended to launch a cold-blooded attack on the West with as much surprise as possible, the General Staff would have a sticky problem in deciding how to balance the necessity for secrecy against the numbers of forces that would be required to carry out a campaign against NATO. Soviet planners have other flanks besides the central front to watch, notably the long border with China and their southern belly, plus their own allies in the Warsaw Pact through whose countries stretch Soviet lines of communication and wherein lie the vast depots required for war. The problem becomes even more complex if there is no concrete decision for war against NATO but instead a series of internal crises that prompt sequential alerts and various stages of mobilization. Nothing is simple in military planning. Threats are everywhere.

Wars never start the way the war game scenarios foresee; the Soviets might be led to the brink of war with conventional forces that had been mobilized for different reasons. In any case, if previous Warsaw Pact crises are any indication, the General Staff could not plan for the successful use of military force without redressing the low readiness status of at least some Soviet and Warsaw Pact ground divisions.

This, then, brings the General Staff to the complexities of its own mobilization system. To achieve maximum surprise with the kind of bolt from the blue associated with worst-case Western scenarios, the Warsaw Pact, including the Soviets, would have to attack with the absolute minimum of mobilization. There are forces immediately available; the GSFG is maintained at a high state of combat readiness, and the other Soviet bloc armies maintain combat-ready forces, particularly the East Germans. Once committed, Soviet planners would know that without full mobilization there would be few forces available to follow up the breakthrough and to carry on the attack deep into NATO's rear. The reservists the USSR relies on to flesh out Category 2 and 3 units are not subjected to any regular military training once they are discharged from active duty. Upon mobilization they are simply gathered up in mass and then parceled out to units in the numbers required. Effective reception, refresher training, and integration are therefore key to how well, and how soon, the unit itself can become combat effective.

As mentioned previously, Soviet Category 3 divisions are maintained in peacetime at levels ranging from cadre to 50 percent strength. Even if they all simultaneously began their fill on M-day, they would be hard pressed to report themselves as combat ready, nor would it seem that the Soviets would regard them as such after only fourteen days or so to receive and integrate their drafts.

Western evidence is contradictory on the subject of how soon the Soviets could begin to move their vital second strategic echelon, and published opinion varies widely. Anthony Cordesman has noted that, "depending on the source, Category 3 units are credited with the ability to achieve readiness in no more than several weeks and often within one week."[4] But another analyst has drawn a different conclusion. According to Jeffrey Record, Category 3 divisions are essentially cadre formations containing only about 25 percent of their manpower and 50 percent of their equipment, most of which is stored. Judged deployable no sooner than M+90 and more likely not until M+120, even completely mobilized Category 3 divisions probably would be seriously deficient in first-line combat equipment and durable logistics support vehicles because the remaining 50 percent of their equipment would have to be obtained from current production, or from stockpiles of older and less reliable equipment.[5]

It is important here to distinguish two issues involving reserve mobilization. Western military thought tends to assign time to train and integrate a newly mobilized unit so that when it is committed its combat power is enhanced by accurately fired weapons, well-maintained vehicles, and coherent leadership. The Soviet military command would probably prefer that route, but it may believe itself pressed simply to move units out as soon as they are assembled, relying on traditional Soviet mass to bring victory. This would result in the arrival of the second strategic echelon on the battlefield much sooner. It also would result in units with low combat effectiveness. Modern tanks and equipment impose their own requirements for maintenance and technical proficiency that could be overlooked in the days of bolt-action rifles and needle bayonets. Additionally, efficient transport of units from rail off-load points (assuming that they are still operating) to staging areas near the front would require considerable expertise on the part of both the transporter and the unit being moved. Loading and unloading armored vehicles on wheeled carriers and convoying the accompanying wheeled support, troops, and ammunition on crowded roads call for a high degree of traffic control knowledge and coordination, neither of which a newly mobilized unit is liable to have. It can probably be done but not efficiently or well. If the Soviets wait to achieve full combat readiness, mobilization is likely to take weeks before the bulk of the divisions can begin moving westward; for instance, from the Belorussian or Kiev military districts.

The best case for the Soviets would be a long mobilization followed by an attack at full strength, but only if the West would stand still and not mobilize in turn. This scenario would grant to the Pact such an overwhelming advantage in strength that surprise might be safely sacrificed, but the West would not stand still. In the thirty to sixty days required for this kind of scenario, both NATO and the Soviets must assume that the West would probably, if belatedly, call up its own reserves. By the time the Pact fully mobilized, the West would be better prepared, with the additional disadvantage to the USSR and its allies that Soviet strategic surprise would have been lost.

In discussing force buildups, some standard of comparison is necessary between Western forces and the forces of the Warsaw Pact. The differences between them are considerable. The standard unit of measurement is an armored division equivalent, based on the standard U.S. armored division as organized in 1980. Using a U.S. armored division as a value of 1.0, a U.S. mechanized division has a value of .94. Other values are as follows:[6]

West German
  Armored division   .72
  Mechanized division   .71

Soviet
  Armored division   .66
  Motorized division   .68

East European
  Armored division   .59
  Motorized rifle division .65

British
  Armored division   .49

French
  Armored division   .30
  Mechanized division   .24

While these figures fluctuate as unit organizations change, they are useful in war gaming, where they are used extensively, and for calculating rough—in some cases very rough—balances. There can be substantial inaccuracies. They do not account, for example, for versatility, leadership, morale, or any of a number of intangible advantages or weaknesses that may mean the difference between victory and defeat. They do illustrate, though, that in comparison to a U.S. division a French one is considerably smaller, and a Soviet one a little more than half strength. Manpower figures are another standard of comparison that must be approached cautiously.[7]

U.S.
    Armored division   18,900
    Mechanized division   18,500

West German
    Armored division   17,000
    Mechanized division   17,500

British
    Armored division   11,500

Soviet
    Armored division   9,500
    Motorized rifle division   12,000

French
    Armored division   7,000
    Mechanized division   6,900

SURPRISE ATTACK

An unreinforced surprise attack—the bolt from the blue—seems the least likely of the two conventional war options, both in military feasibility and in terms of political profit and risk for the Soviets. From a purely military point of view, the USSR could conceivably mount a surprise attack with its own forces that could achieve a considerable initial military success. Force ratios are irrelevant because NATO forces are not deployed or prepared to resist in the initial stages, having only scattered border reconnaissance elements to oppose a first assault. P. H. Vigor has postulated a 20-division, all-Soviet attack at midnight on Christmas Day along the North German Plain, running roughly from Magdeburg past Hannover and assisted by Soviet airborne and helicopter-borne forces as well as by air and fifth-column forces.[8] In his scenario, in which he acknowledges having given both sides several best-case assumptions, the head of the Soviet blitz is in the vicinity of Hannover by 4:00 A.M., a considerable accomplishment for a night attack, even one that has met minimal resistance and has been able to keep to the roads.

Given Vigor's assumptions, such a scenario seems militarily plausible. Provided that complete surprise is achieved, execution is within the capability of the GSFG, which is organized virtually as an autonomous offensive force. Another study of NATO's ability to survive such an attack gives the Pact another 10 divisions after four days of mobilization but concludes that, in a 30-division attack against an unreinforced NATO total of 30⅓ divisions, barring any NATO tactical blunders, the Pact forces would have a very low probability of achieving a significant breakthrough. Should the allies make mistakes (misjudging the direction of the Pact main attack, for instance, or failing to respond to strategic warning), then the likelihood of a Warsaw Pact breakthrough increases precipitously to 80 percent.[9] But such an attack's operational feasibility is not matched on the strategic level. Because of low force levels, operationally the 20-division attack would have to be assigned limited objectives no deeper than 100 kilometers.[10] The 30-division attack would not fare much better, although it might succeed in cutting the main U.S. north-south line of communications.

Worldwide reaction would be incalculable. Even with unreinforced forces, NATO could then threaten to pinch off the attacking force. Even if it reached its objectives within twenty-four hours, the attacking force would come under tremendous pressure as NATO got itself sorted out, as Soviet combat units and logistics were attacked by Western air power, and, most importantly, the unmobilized Soviets would be unable to reinforce or replace their forward units, leaving the Soviets with a difficult strategic equation involving defeat, nuclear weapons, or negotiation. If the attack is launched in darkness, effective use of Soviet close support air power to blast allied defenses is made more difficult. Since secrecy would be so vital, the Pact's air forces would not have moved to dispersed fields and thereby would be vulnerable to allied counterair strikes. Other disadvantages would accrue to the

Soviet air forces such as an unwillingness to mass aircraft formations in the air prior to the initial strike. After daybreak, air support of Soviet Ground Forces would be more feasible, but by then the allied air forces would have been fully alerted, and the NATO counterair campaign would be, one assumes, in full swing.

Operational questions aside, the most significant objection to an unreinforced attack is the idea that it could be mounted with no strategic warning. There would be no period of tension, no large-scale mobilization within the USSR, and no indication through the East European countries of a Warsaw Pact movement or involvement. It assumes that the Soviets would be willing to risk not informing or mobilizing their allies and to try to shift a great nation overnight, without warning, from normal peacetime operations to a war footing complete with effective mobilization and fully coordinated logistic operations. Not even the Prussians at the height of their power were capable of such action. Even the Kremlin's more adventurous military operations, such as the Czechoslovak invasion and the present Afghan intervention, were undertaken only after the leadership was assured of a threat to the USSR on its own border, convinced of a low probability of U.S. military opposition, and after a mobilization period that was detected and reported by the West. One analyst has calculated that the Soviets need about three months to mount an attack,[11] a reasonable reaction of professional military men in an organization prone to foul-ups.[12] Soviet leaders, especially the military elite, are probably well aware of their own weaknesses. Benjamin Lambeth has pointed out that "it seems reasonable to suggest that these elements of anxiety and uncertainty could exert a powerful self-deterrence in future crises short of one where Soviet decision-makers were *so convinced that a major war was coming that some decisive preemptive move was required.*"[13]

It then seems logical and prudent to assume that, if war were to come to the central front, it would probably not come from a single crisis that sprang up overnight but from a series of crises that multiplied the decisions and problems and magnified the errors of decision makers on both sides. In his study of surprise attack, Richard Betts has described a scenario that he refers to as a political version of the "Titanic coincidence," in which a series of minor coincidences pile up to overwhelm predictable outcomes. Betts claims that on the central front "the greater danger is a situation of multiple unlikely crises that aggravate each other and overload the brake systems, where deterioration begins to appear out of control and the structure of deterrence appears to be collapsing."[14] Given the stakes involved in central Europe, which intimately involve the national survival of all participants, the multiple crisis scenario of rising tensions and eroding control seems more valid than one of a sudden Soviet decision to go to war. It is valid enough that planning for conventional defense can be postulated on at least some strategic warning. What NATO chooses to do with that warning is another question.

PARTIAL MOBILIZATION

For definition, "partial mobilization" applies to both sides in the early stages of full mobilization, or, having begun a limited mobilization, to address a situation not having to do with all-out war. For NATO, partial mobilization can only be conducted in response to a perceived Warsaw Pact threat. As mentioned earlier, Pact forces, however, may partially mobilize to deal with domestic problems as well as a NATO threat, leaving NATO uncertain about their ultimate intentions.

The Pact's mobilization pattern would vary depending on the immediate task at hand, and in later stages by how the Soviet leaders read NATO's response. For example, if events along the Chinese border concerned the Kremlin, then, as a reassuring signal to the West, it might deliberately not mobilize the 22 divisions in the Kiev and Carpathian military districts. Trouble in the East European countries might trigger call-ups of the divisions in the Belorussian and Baltic districts, or in selected divisions throughout all the western districts.

NATO's OPTIONS

The most crucial issue for NATO would be the beginning of mobilization and reinforcement. Soviet mobilization would have to be perceived as sufficiently serious to alarm the West into taking decisive action. Western leaders would know that the economic effect of mobilization on the USSR would potentially be more burdensome than on the West. The Soviet civilian labor force would be cut severely, and the aid normally given by the military sector to civilian production would be lost. Still, the disruption of ordinary Western economic and social life also would be enormous. It is quite easy to assume that the NATO Defense Planning Committee (DPC), a coordinating body of fourteen voting national representatives, would be unwilling to take the required steps until the Soviet mobilization had become too obvious to ignore.

Estimating NATO's reaction to a Soviet mobilization is the more difficult task because no official NATO alert or mobilization has ever been called. Operational commanders do have some latitude over alert status—but not mobilization—for their forces, the lowest being *military vigilance*, which can be declared by senior NATO military commanders. Above military vigilance, approval for moving to the stages of *simple alert*, *reinforced alert*, and *general alert* is required from the DPC, whose reaction, particularly to something as serious as mobilization, is unpredictable. The need for early decisions on reinforcement, deployment, and call-up would be absolutely critical in the peace-to-war stage, both to prepare for the worst and to deter Soviet ambitions. An analysis of the time required for NATO to move forces already in Europe into position for maximum preparedness, including erecting obstacles, digging in, and zeroing artillery, indicates that about one week would be required.[15]

There are several crisis levels even after mobilization has begun. European mobilization might well be conducted hesitantly; the filling and movement of Dutch units to their defensive positions along the IGB might be carried out at a comparatively low key. The German Territorial Army units likewise might fill under similar conditions.

A major threshold of NATO's reaction, in addition to European mobilization, would be the decision to begin U.S. reinforcement of Europe, with American units being deployed from bases within the United States to prepositioned equipment in Europe. Simultaneously, a limited, and then a general, call-up of American reserve forces would be required to handle the deployment and to begin the fill of National Guard and reserve units that would follow the active forces.

The third and final level of preparedness would involve the evacuation of civilians from certain areas including the redeployment of U.S. and other allied dependents within the Federal Republic; the occupation of defensive positions; and the consequent destruction of civilian property as barriers were built, firing positions sited, and artillery preregistered. All of these plateaus, or "firebreaks," would call for separate NATO decisions; there would be many others. Unless the Soviet and Pact threat were universally perceived, it seems reasonable to expect some hesitation on the part of the DPC. In fact, the chances that NATO would be able to achieve political unanimity on these grave points is questionable and leads pessimists to the view that the Alliance could not react in time to the kind of Soviet mobilization postulated here.

There is another option. NATO's authorization is not the only way that Western forces can be brought to combat readiness. Without a DPC decision, the member nations of NATO retain the authority to mobilize in their own right, which could easily lead to a scenario in which individual states begin mobilization. In this regard, the key nations are obviously the biggest ones: the United States, the Federal Republic, France, and Britain. Given the U.S. goal of moving 6 divisions, 1 MAB, and 60 tactical fighter squadrons in Europe within ten days, the U.S.-West German tie is critical.[16] The Federal Republic's reserves can be "on line" in forty-eight hours; likewise, the main body of British reinforcement of British I Corps is due to arrive within seventy-two hours and is key to a successful defense of the Northern Army Group (NORTHAG), especially if the Dutch and Belgians are slow to mobilize and fill their sectors in the vital center. The French are a special case and will be discussed below.

The interface during the mobilization period between the political and military leaderships on both sides of the IGB would be dominated by demands for political control and constant reevaluations of the military balance. For the West, mobilization is liable to proceed smoothly only as long as the military can convince the civilian leadership that control is being maintained over the mobilization/escalation ladder, and that by mobilizing the West has not begun an irrevocable slide toward war. At this point, the difference in NATO and Pact military doctrine becomes critically important. NATO can achieve its objectives by simply standing still; the Pact, if it follows its doctrine, must achieve a sufficient advantage in forces and surprise if an attack is likely to succeed. If NATO's mobilization stalemates the Pact and frustrates its doctrinal preemptive move, then NATO "wins."

THE WARSAW PACT'S REACTIONS

Warsaw Pact reaction to Western initiatives depends very much on the situation and the way in which the Kremlin views the NATO threat. Certainly the arrival of strong U.S. armored formations, the call-up of German reservists, and the French reaction would tend to reinforce the Soviet perception that the world is ganging up on the USSR. The critical point is liable to be when the General Staff calculates the correlation of forces. If it sees a doubtful outcome, then the recommendation to the political leadership may well be to do nothing. If the balance too definitely favors the West, all other things considered, the Soviet General Staff may still recommend doing nothing, or reaching for the nuclear trigger, which would be a political nonoption if Western nuclear deterrence has been maintained. If the West has lagged too far behind, and the option is to press the advantage while it exists, then the decision may be for war, although the Soviet mobilization is not as complete as the General Staff would prefer.

Assuming that the Warsaw Pact decides to attack after about two weeks of mobilization, in which NATO lags by four days to one week, what are the probabilities of a Pact breakthrough? After fourteen days the Soviet Union would have available about 86 tank and motorized rifle divisions—the first strategic echelon—that could be used to attack the central front. The sources of these divisions bear mentioning.[17] Thirty are Category 1 Soviet divisions stationed in Eastern Europe, and 22 are other Warsaw Pact national divisions (20 Category 1 and 2 Category 2). Within the Soviet Union the Baltic, Belorussian, and Carpathian military districts would provide 4 Category 1 and 30 Category 2 divisions. Seven Category 3 Pact divisions would remain behind, mobilizing. There also would be 6 Soviet Category 1 airborne divisions and 1 Polish airborne division available for use against rear areas and as a strategic reserve, but these divisions would probably remain under the control of the Soviet High Command.

Behind the first strategic echelon, once the decision had been made for, or events had led to, open hostilities, mobilization of the remaining Soviet and Pact divisions would be under way. In this partial mobilization scenario, the assumption is made that the first strategic echelon has closed on NATO along the IGB; that all forces will be used in the attack, leaving none to secure LOCs; that the battle would be concentrated in the north; and that all divisions, including the Pact and Soviet Category 2 divisions that would mobilize and move with 50 percent new personnel, are all at full combat effectiveness. These assumptions give a best-case capability to the Pact that may not be entirely realistic.

OPENING THE GAP

Recalling that this scenario began with a partial mobilization, there is now a gap between the first strategic echelon, which mobilized at M-day and has closed on NATO's forward defenses, and the second echelon, which began mobilizing about one week later. However, even if it had begun filling at the same time, there would still be a gap because these are Category 3 units, and their work-up would take longer than forces already committed. The divisions in the second strategic echelon consist of Category 3 units: probably 26 from the Baltic, Belorussian, and Carpathian military districts; 17 from the Kiev and Moscow districts, thus tapping the Central Strategic Reserve; and 10 Category 3 East European divisions, for a total of 53 divisions. Because of the delay caused by activation, and because they have to come through Eastern Europe in the face of NATO deep attacks, their attrition during movement from air attacks, providing air is available to employ against them, and simple breakdowns can be expected to be high.

Recognizing that the exact divisional totals are problematic, the picture now for a partial mobilization scenario would be of a roughly 90-division attack going in against NATO at around M+14 (mobilization plus fourteen days). In the Soviet Union another 40+ divisions are "standing up," with 10 trying to do so in Eastern Europe. Assuming that both sides at this point will see no advantage in using nuclear weapons, the closure of the second frontal echelon of forces on the battlefield must be a major preoccupation for the Soviet General

Staff. Its decision will depend in large measure on the success of reinforcement in the West.

REINFORCEMENT AND CONGESTION

In strategists' language, D-day in this scenario would equal Soviet M-day plus fourteen ($D = M + 14$). For the West, with a one-week delay, $D = M + 7$. (If NATO countries mobilized individually, then there would be a hodgepodge of M-days and different equations. The differences are too complex to track here, except to try to aggregate the total effect.)

Under partial mobilization, so long as the West does not lag by more than about one week, geography works in its favor. European reserves mobilize near the areas in which they will be employed, while Soviet forces have to be moved across Eastern Europe to the front. To about $D + 20$, NATO should be able to deny the Soviets the quantitative advantage they need for assured victory.

The amount of forces NATO can employ after about seven days' mobilization is critical. There are currently 26 NATO combat divisions and 8 brigades or regiments in the central region, for an estimated total of $28+$ divisional groupings.[18] By $M+4$, NATO can muster $30+$ maneuver divisions in the central region, not counting West German territorial brigades and other home-guard units; by $M+9$ the number could increase to 43, not including U.S. reinforcements.[19] A second mobilization study concludes that NATO could muster 35 division equivalents by $M+7$.[20] With 6 U.S. divisions currently planned and budgeted to fall in on POMCUS, the number of NATO divisions available for combat two weeks after mobilization began, and one week after hostilities commenced, would go up another 2 or 3, as some U.S. units would have completed the process of arrival, equipment draw, and movement.[21]

An assumption is made here that the United States is not involved in any other deployments, such as the movement of the Rapid Deployment Force to the Mideast, which would divert air and sealift from the flow of forces to Europe. If 3 U.S. divisions were detained on a mission in the Mideast, the U.S. Congressional Budget Office has estimated that the overall East-West force ratio on the central front after four weeks of mobilization would be 1.8:1 rather than 1.7:1.[22] The most immediate effect of U.S. involvement in another theater prior to, or simultaneously with, a NATO alert would be on strategic lift. Europe would receive priority, but there probably would be some reinforcement delay caused by reorientation of strategic lift assets.[23] It is a safe assumption that any other theater would quickly become secondary if mobilization began in Europe.

Assuming no competitive U.S. deployment, Table 5 illustrates the approximate central region balance by M+7. Deployment and attrition of air power would be crucial for maintenance of air superiority, for attack of Soviet nuclear weapons sites and units, for interdiction of Soviet and Pact units approaching the battlefield, and for close air support of forward units. Certainly allied airfields and aircraft on the ground would be prime targets for Soviet air and perhaps ground-to-ground conventional missiles, especially for the first air campaign on D-day. Airfield vulnerability is increased by its proximity to East Germany, but that situation can be offset to some degree, although not completely satisfactorily from the logistics point of view, if France would open its bases at or after mobilization.

It is at least reasonable to assume that the Soviets would try to cripple allied air power in the first hours of an attack. How well they would do depends on a number of imponderables. One is the competence of allied leadership. It can be assumed that NATO will not offer up its bases undefended and its aircraft parked wing tip to wing tip, as in the Philippines in December 1941. With any kind of premobilization, it is safe to assume that aircraft would be dispersed and base defenses at a higher stage of alert. A second imponderable is the weather; a third is the time of day. Overarching all is the competence of Warsaw Pact pilots and the accuracy of their air-to-ground and ground-to-ground missiles. (If they risk missiles, such action might be misconstrued as a nuclear attack.) All this is highly speculative. One study concludes:

> As part of its blitzkrieg strategy, the Pact might well attempt to accompany its ground attack with a large-scale offensive against NATO air bases and nuclear capabilities. Because of low kill probabilities, poor maintenance and allied air defenses, this attack would probably damage no

Table 5. NATO and Warsaw Pact Ground Forces at M+14

	M-day	M+7	M+14 (D-day)
Warsaw Pact			
Soviet Union	19	26	59
East Germany	6	6	6
Czechoslovakia	6	8[a]	8
Poland	–	5[b]	10[c]
D-day Total Divisions:			83[d]
NATO			
Belgium	⅔	2⅔	2⅓
Britain	4⅓	5	5
Canada	⅓	⅓	⅓[e]
Denmark	1	1⅔	1
France	3	7	7[f]
Netherlands	⅓	3	2
United States	5⅔	7	9
West Germany	12	14	15⅓[g]
D-day Total Divisions:			42

[a] Assumes 2 Category 2 divisions are filled and ready at M+4.
[b] Assumes movement of a portion of Poland's Category 1 divisions to the IGB by M+7.
[c] Includes all of Poland's Category 1 and 2 divisions.
[d] Kaufmann, in "Nuclear Deterrence in Central Europe," in Steinbruner and Segal, *Alliance Security*, p. 60, comes up with a total of 90 divisions. The difference seems to be in the Czech and Polish Category 3 divisions; he counts them, but I do not. It seems illogical that Pact Category 3 units, in view of their obvious low combat status, would be given movement priority sufficiently high to get them to the front in fourteen days.
[e] There are opposing views of Canada's intent to reinforce its European brigade. This is the low estimate. See Mako, *U.S. Ground Forces*, p. 50; and Kaufmann, "Nuclear Deterrence in Central Europe," in Steinbruner and Segal, *Alliance Security*, p. 62.
[f] Assumes France comes in at or near NATO M-day and commits another corps of 4 divisions to support the 1 already in Germany, leaving 5 additional armored and mechanized divisions immediately available.
[g] Includes the 6 Territorial Army heavy brigades, which here are aggregated roughly into 1⅓ division equivalents, although they contain a total of 12 tank battalions and 12 infantry battalions. The total count does not address the 6 light home-guard brigades and 15 home-guard regiments, plus other security.
Sources: Author's notes; and Mako, *U.S. Ground Forces*, p. 51; and Kaufmann, "Nuclear Deterrence in Central Europe," in Steinbruner and Segal, *Alliance Security*, pp. 60–62. Reprinted by permission of Brookings Institution. See also *Military Balance, 1983–1984*, pp. 14–35; and *DoD 1984 Budget*, p. 215.

more than 30 per cent of an estimated 19,300 targets and collapse after about five days. . . . NATO more or less simultaneously would be committing roughly 16 per cent of its offensive aircraft to close air support and the remaining 84 per cent to the deep missions of air superiority, nuclear suppression, and interdiction.[24]

Given the present superiority of U.S. and NATO aircraft and warning systems, NATO should be able to gain air superiority in local sectors for short periods during the early post-D-day stages. The really contentious NATO air power decision in the early days after hostilities began would be whether to invest in close air support in order to relieve hard-pressed ground units, a move that would pay immediate benefits, or to go after deep targets with strikes whose effect would not be apparent for two to three weeks. Allocation of air sorties between these two roles would play a crucial part in preventing a Soviet breakthrough.

Mobilization estimates of the air order of battle are shown on Table 6. Soviet air defense aircraft are not counted, and M-day is Soviet M-day. Aircraft attrition would be a difficult problem for NATO air planners, but, at least in the early phases of the war, there would be sufficient planes and crews deploying from the United States to maintain a reasonable balance.

Given the number of divisions and amount of air support that NATO could expect to muster after seven days' mobilization, a broad front Pact attack would play into the West's hands since NATO forces are spread generally evenly along the border.[25] But, since the Pact knows it would probably not gain a decisive advantage, it almost surely would choose another course of action to achieve its goal as fast as possible. Its most profitable option, and one in keeping with Pact doctrine, would be to attack defensively along much of the IGB and to concentrate its effort in the sectors where it can achieve high enough force ratios to obtain a decisive breakthrough. Given terrain constraints, the south of Europe is not an attractive sector for a major push since the mountainous countryside impedes the kind of rapid advance that the Soviets seek, and France's location gives the defenders considerable depth on which to fall back. The extreme northern parts of Germany, at the neck of the Danish peninsula, are likewise not suitable for rapid armor advance because of boggy ground, rivers, and

Table 6. NATO and Pact Aircraft Reinforcement

	M-day		M+14	
	Attack	Fighter	Attack	Fighter
Warsaw Pact				
Soviet Union	770	500	1780	1850
East Germany	47	300	47	300
Czechoslovakia	164	252	164	252
Poland	220	430	220	430
D-day Total:			2211	2832
NATO[a]				
Belgium	90	36	90	36
Britain	180	183	180	207
Canada	24	54[b]	24	54
Denmark	72	32	72	32
France	225	149	248	149
Netherlands	72	54	72	54
United States	258	264	600	640[c]
West Germany	324	60	372	60
D-day Total:			1658	1232

[a]NATO figures do not include operational conversion units of aircraft planned for conversion from training roles to tactical missions.
[b]Reflects purchase of CF-18s.
[c]Figure represents NATO reinforced by about 40 squadrons. Extrapolated from FY 1984 budget objective of reinforcing Europe with 60 squadrons in ten days. U.S. and NATO squadrons flying F-16s were counted as listed in *Military Balance, 1983–1984*, although aircraft can fly dual-attack and air superiority missions.

Sources: Modeled after Kaufmann, "Nuclear Deterrence in Central Europe," in Steinbruner and Segal, *Alliance Security*, p. 77; updated with *Military Balance, 1983–1984*. Soviet figures are extremely difficult to judge because of the USSR's security concerns in its Far Eastern and Southern theaters. Soviet air defense aircraft are not reflected.

the built-up areas around Hamburg. The North German Plain, however, offers solid and reasonably flat ground, although with considerable urban sprawl. Making the best of bad choices, the Soviets and their allies should be expected, with minimum forces, to hold the extreme northern front at the neck of Denmark, concentrate for a major attack opposite Hannover, and then mount two smaller supporting offensives at Fulda and Hof in the south. The forces in between would attempt to maintain the offensive tactically, but strategically they would be performing a defensive or static role. (This assumes that no opportunity for a decisive breakthrough occurs elsewhere on the front which would reorient Soviet and NATO forces.)

The critical areas for NATO defense therefore would be, in order, the North German Plain in the vicinity of Hannover, the south in the area of the Fulda Gap and the Hof Corridor, and points in between. In the seven days, more or less, of mobilization, the forces assigned to those critical regions and elsewhere on the front would have arrived in position, and some limited defensive preparation should have begun. NATO is believed to require between forty-eight and ninety-six hours to occupy its forward defense positions.[26]

In the critical North German Plain sector, opposite the Soviet 3d Shock Army and the 2d Guards Tank Army (see Diagram 2), the British, Dutch, and Belgian forces would have come up just north of the Harz Mountains to contest the Soviet attack on Hannover.[27] NATO forces in these corps sectors would total about 10 divisions of various compositions, plus elements probably of 2 or 3 home-guard brigades or regiments.[28] With 30 regular brigades in the 4 NORTHAG corps sectors, and allowing one-third back in reserve, one study has concluded that each brigade would have about an 8-kilometer front to cover, which is a satisfactory brigade frontage, especially with help from obstacles and Territorial Army units, if available.[29] The terrain is densely built up, restricting to a degree the movement of vehicles and providing cover and concealment for defending forces (see Map 4).

Western forces would incur several other advantages. First, they would be fighting on home ground and on the defensive. The enormous disruption of command and communication systems on both sides would favor the defender, who only has to stand and fight. Second, in this scenario the Pact has failed to gain strategic, and probably tactical, surprise, with all the attendant benefits to the West. Third, NATO forces would be fighting and falling back on their own logistic bases and manpower pools, which are considerable. If used methodically, these national pools of individual replacements could help offset attrition within combat units and the maintenance of combat power as Warsaw Pact units are ground down.

There is also a question of the Soviets' ability to maintain tactical maneuverability as they mass for a breakthrough in the congested urban and built-up areas of Western Europe.

SURPRISE AND MOBILIZATION

Diagram 2[a]

NATO Combat Units on the Central Front[b]

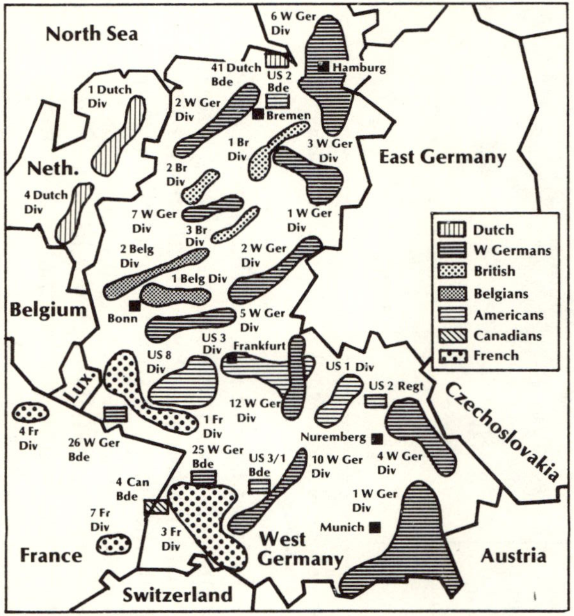

Soviet Forces on the Central Front[c]

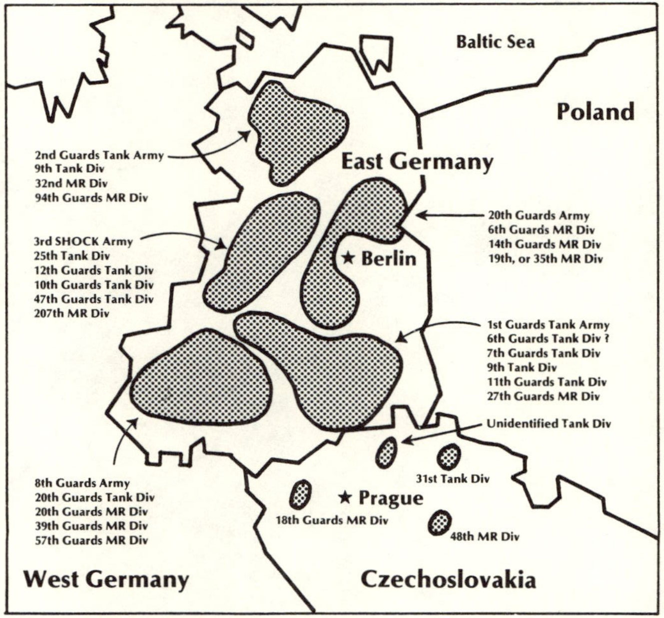

[a] Approximate locations are based on late 1981 estimates by Phillip A. Karber.
[b] Adapted from *The Economist*, 31 July 1982, p. 31.
[c] Adapted from John Collins, *The NATO Warsaw Pact Balance*, Congressional Research Service, 1980. Five Soviet Divisions are directly subordinate to the Czech Group of Forces. The 30th Guards Motor Rifle (MR) near Zvolen is off the map in eastern Czechoslovakia.
Source: Anthony J. Cordesman, "The NATO Central Region and the Balance of Uncertainty," *Armed Forces Journal* 120, no. 12 (July 1983): 40. Reprinted by permission of Anthony Cordesman and the *Armed Forces Journal*.

Map 4. Built-up Areas in West Germany

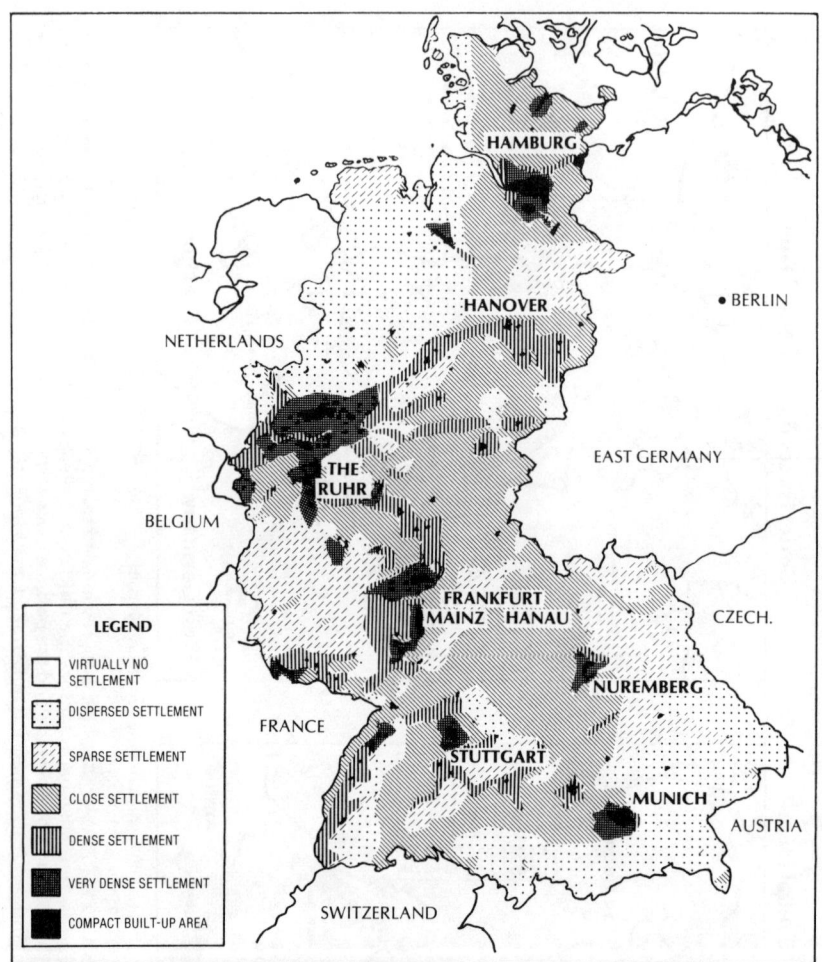

Source: Department of the Army, *FM 100-5, Operations* (Washington, DC: Government Printing Office, 1982), p. 3–9.

It should be noted that the issue of battlefield congestion is a tactical, or operational, question, one having little to do with the question of whether the Pact would attack on a broad or narrow front in the north or south. If the Alliance successfully took advantage of the attacker's jammed-in tactical formations, however, the eventual effect would be strategic, feeding back from the tactical and operational loss of maneuver and speed so vital to the Soviets' success.

As an example of frontage congestion at the tactical and operational level, a Soviet motorized or tank battalion, in accordance with Pact doctrine, would attack on a front of 1 to 2 kilometers, with each company sector about 500 to 800 meters wide.[30] Two companies would lead the assault, with the battalion's third company following closely as a second tactical echelon, or reserve, and then that battalion followed closely by a second battalion.

In a sand table display or training area, such a mass of armor rolling forward seems irresistible. It is a formidable threat, but anyone who actually has ever had to maneuver armor across country and through built-up areas knows it is not the smooth and rapid evolution shown on the sand table. Instead there are rapid spurts across open areas. Then there is the maneuvering through streets and over embankments, then stream gullies and stone walls, all the while trying to keep one's own tanks in sight and to look for those of the enemy. Compound the scene by adding air attack, noise, smoke, and unfriendly fire, thereby driving formations off the roads and into the fields and forests. Visual contact would be lost, both with guiding roads and with friends. Units on narrow fronts would wander into the paths of neighboring formations. The Red Army's problems are further increased with its reluctance to train tank crews in map reading or land navigation.

Soviet doctrine calls for cities and built-up areas to be bypassed where possible. The North German Plain, however, is replete with urban buildup that would channelize movement, although with a little time competent defenders could improve on natural channelization. Clusters of buildings and highways would hinder maneuverability and vision, especially when the hulks of destroyed or broken down vehicles block previously opened lines of advance if accurate fire is falling and if vehicle crews are driving below hatches with restricted views and all the other disadvantages that causes. If opposed by skillful defense with sufficient firepower to disrupt Soviet capabilities to plan, act, and react to changing tactical situations, then the weight and inflexibility of the Soviet attack becomes a serious disadvantage as units pile up and the rigid command structure overloads trying to sort things out. In an analysis of the central region conventional balance, Barry Posen, Rockefeller Foundation International Affairs Fellow at Georgetown University, has cited the World War II case of an attacking U.S. corps that attempted a concentration of forces similar to that assumed by Soviet doctrine. The corps was so cramped that part of the attacking force had to be withheld until more space could be opened by the advance, and this in conditions of total air superiority against an enemy very short on ammunition.[31]

In this kind of situation, applying Soviet versus Western *force-to-space* against *force-to-force* ratios in a variety of conditions, Posen has found that the most favorable attacker-versus-defender ratio that the Soviets achieve is 2.25:1. When he applies tactical air power to each side, the ratio drops to 2:1, or even 1.4:1, depending on assumptions. Either figure is below the attacker-defender ratio that both NATO and the Soviets believe necessary for a Pact breakthrough.[32] However, the West's more flexible command arrangements and policy of "initiative forward" would enable local commanders to take advantage of Pact dependence on centralized control. A former U.S. Air Force fighter pilot calls this getting "inside" the adversary's observation-orientation-decision-action time cycle.[33]

The sum of this argument is that the Soviet attack on the northern plain would have serious problems, even today. The picture that emerges is a far cry from the Soviet doctrinal expectation of achieving a high rate of advance every day. Barring serious NATO tactical or operational blunders, there is a reasonable expectation, with one week of NATO mobilization before D-day, of significantly slowing, if not stopping, an initial Soviet attack conducted from a partially mobilized base.

There is, though, the danger that Western tactical blunders or Pact dispositions could result in a breach of NATO defensive positions and a Soviet breakthrough into NATO's rear. No more serious conventional threat could be posed than a group of Soviet armored divisions loose behind NATO's front, aided by Soviet airmobile or parachute troops attacking the vulnerable logistics, communications, and command systems located behind the main line of contact.

In this case, only strong armored reserves located in the area of the breakthrough can hope to halt and ultimately defeat large armored formations. The Territorial Army of the Federal Republic, plus whatever other light units are present and the logistic troops in the area, can provide no more than point defense of selected targets. At present, a U.S. corps to be deployed from the United States is planned as NORTHAG reserve.[34] CENTAG reserve would be provided by the Canadian Brigade Group and, if France enters the war, by the First French Army. While these forces in and of themselves are excellent, the NORTHAG Corps is permanently stationed in the United States (less a brigade stationed in Europe), and the CENTAG force either belongs to France, and would probably be committed only under national control,[35] or, in the case of the Canadian brigade, is first-class but too small. Above the level of the Army Group commanders, the commander of AFCENT has no reserves at all. This paucity, or, in AFCENT's case, lack of reserves, is the most troubling aspect of NATO's present dispositions.

THE RACE TO REINFORCE

A constant counterpoint to the progress of the actual battles on the central front would be the arrival and disposition of NATO reinforcements and the mobilization and movement of Soviet divisions from the Baltic, Belorussian, and Carpathian military districts, as well as from points east. The overwhelming majority of these units are Category 3. The Soviet leadership would be aware that, once the Category 3 divisions are committed, there would be no second chance to hold them back and fully prepare them for maximum effectiveness. Thus the decision facing the Soviet High Command would be to use either less effective units faster, or more effective units too late.

The arrival on the battlefield of the second strategic echelon would be the last hope that the Soviet leadership would have of the quick victory dictated by its doctrine. Simultaneously with the movement of the second echelon of forces and with all the actions discussed thus far, the Soviets would be conducting national mobilization, raising new divisions, withdrawing from storage the masses of old equipment they have saved through the decades, and preparing fresh divisions to begin movement toward the front.

These actions are well beyond the first thirty days of war and, in fact, would signify a strategic defeat for the Kremlin as it would then be embarked on the kind of war its economic structure can least afford, one against a coalition that has the advantage of both greater manpower and economic resources. No mention has been made yet regarding the disposition of those considerable Soviet forces in the Far East. How the Soviets would regard China at this point is beyond conjecture, although it seems certain that they would not leave that long border unguarded. This would be the "moment of truth" for the Soviet leadership and also the more difficult because the realization would come upon it incrementally that it would now appear to have only three options.

The first would be to try to use nuclear weapons to cause a change in the correlation of forces. But, if the nuclear correlation has remained roughly equal, or if it favors the West, and if there has been no catastrophic loss on the battlefield to threaten the existence of the Soviet Union, then recourse to nuclear weapons should remain an undesirable option. Second, the Kremlin could continue the war in hopes that something would turn up, but this is also less than desirable. Believing in the correlation of forces themselves, the Soviets could see the tide turning against them. Finally, the third option would be to negotiate to save the Soviet state. This seems to be the most desirable choice since it offers the best hope of preserving the authority and integrity of the USSR. It may be even more desirable if the war was unintentional from the start. At this point—beyond thirty days of war—trying to forecast Pact or Western actions could not be anything but conjecture, as the world would be enormously changed beyond anything known today. In a military sense, however, NATO would have achieved a measure of success. The Alliance would have survived and done so without crossing the nuclear threshold. The allies would be turning their minds toward the next steps. Furthermore, for NATO to have the capability to reach this point would be the best insurance possible that it would never be necessary to do so.

Notes

[1] Paul Bracken, "The NATO Defense Problem," *Orbis* 27, no. 1 (Spring 1983): 89.

[2] A scenario that assumes no Western reaction to Soviet mobilization leads to NATO's defeat. The real question is not whether NATO would mobilize but how long the Alliance can delay once the Soviets begin.

SURPRISE AND MOBILIZATION 111

³Fred C. Ikle, *Every War Must End* (New York: Columbia University Press, 1971), p. 8.

⁴Anthony J. Cordesman, "The NATO Central Region and the Balance of Uncertainty," *Armed Forces Journal* 120, no. 12 (July 1983): 36.

⁵Record, *Sizing Up the Soviet Army*, p. 22. This is the point made in Chapter Three. Record's view would be more militarily prudent than Cordesman's if the objective were to be a war of several campaigns and longer duration than the Soviets' doctrine envisions. The urgency with which the Soviets could be expected to reinforce their forward units as a result of their doctrine, however, and their traditional emphasis on mass, lend credibility to the view that they would not take time to bring units to Western standards of operational readiness.

⁶Mako, *U.S. Ground Forces*, pp. 114–25. U.S. armored and mechanized forces are in the process of reorganization.

⁷Figures are taken from ibid., p. 113; and Collins, *Military Balance*, p. 489. These figures assume that the same values apply to Soviet and other Warsaw Pact units. Mako and Collins assume that Warsaw Pact forces are generally the same as Soviet.

⁸Vigor, *Soviet Blitzkrieg Theory*, pp. 183–205.

⁹Kaufmann, "Nuclear Deterrence in Central Europe," in Steinbruner and Segal, *Alliance Security*, pp. 64–66.

¹⁰Jonathan Alford, "Perspectives on Strategy," ibid., p. 97.

¹¹Kaufmann, quoted in Betts, *Surprise Attack*, p. 8.

¹²Suvorov, *Inside the Soviet Army*, pp. 215–87.

¹³Benjamin S. Lambeth, "Uncertainties for the Soviet War Planner," *International Security* 7, No. 3 (Winter 1982–83): 145 (emphasis added).

¹⁴Betts, *Surprise Attack*, p. 158. In 1946, Brodie, in *Absolute Weapon*, p. 74, wrote: "The fear that one's country might suddenly be attacked in the midst of apparently profound peace has often been voiced, but, at least in the last century and a half, it has never been realized. . . . In international politics today few things are more certain than an attack must have an antecedent hostility of obviously grave character." There is no apparent reason to challenge Brodie's statement today.

¹⁵Betts, *Surprise Attack*, p. 173. It is difficult to estimate maximum preparedness in terms of days. Even one or two days of combat engineer preparation could turn an urban area into an effective obstacle.

¹⁶*DoD 1984 Budget*, p. 209. The 1984 forecast included initial support units.

¹⁷Mako, *U.S. Ground Forces*, p. 44; and *Military Balance, 1983–1984*, p. 16.

¹⁸The Danish and West German divisions assigned to Allied Forces Northern Europe (AFNORTH) are counted here.

¹⁹Kaufmann, "Nuclear Deterrence in Central Europe," in Steinbruner and Segal, *Alliance Security*, p. 62.

²⁰Mako, *U.S. Ground Forces*, p. 54.

²¹*DoD 1984 Budget*, pp. 215–16.

²²Congressional Budget Office, *Army Ground Combat Modernization in the 1980s: Potential Costs and Effects for NATO* (Washington, DC: Government Printing Office, 1982), p. 31–32.

²³Collins, *Military Balance*, p. 188.

²⁴Kaufmann, "Nuclear Deterrence in Central Europe," in Steinbruner and Segal, *Alliance Security*, p. 76.

²⁵Mearsheimer, "Why the Soviets Can't Win Quickly in Central Europe," pp. 18–19.

²⁶Cordesman, "The NATO Central Region and the Balance of Uncertainty," p. 40.

²⁷There will have been sufficient time to move and emplace the Dutch. In this scenario NATO members are assumed to be supporting the Alliance, although with some time for national debate, and the Soviets are granted the unconstrained support of their allies, including the mobilization and employment of Pact Category 2 divisions.

²⁸Mako, *U.S. Ground Forces*, p. 51.

[29] Mearsheimer, "Why the Soviets Can't Win Quickly in Central Europe," p. 28. Note that Barry Posen's study (see note 31 below) also discusses various defensive strength calculations, pp. 119–20.

[30] Department of the Army, *Soviet Military Operations* (Washington, DC: Government Printing Office, 1980), p. 3–84.

[31] Barry Posen, "Competing Views of the Central Region Conventional Balance," in Keith A. Dunn and William O. Staudenmaier, eds., *Alternative Military Strategies for the Future* (Boulder, CO: Westview, 1984), p. 123.

[32] Ibid.

[33] John R. Boyd, "Patterns of Conflict" (briefing prepared on tempo of warfare, September 1981).

[34] Mearsheimer, "Why the Soviets Can't Win Quickly in Central Europe," p. 23.

[35] Peter J. Berger, "The Course of French Defense Policy," *Parameters* 22, no. 3 (September 1982): 24.

Chapter Five

Realigning Conventional Strategy

GOOD STRATEGIC PLANNING should give a commander the most effective concentration of his forces and maximum freedom of action. At the strategic level, planning specifically for how a war is to be fought is in the best case merely wasted effort and, in the worst case, disastrous. Plans should reflect aims, a general concept of overall intentions, then identify initial actions designed to gain an advantageous position as early as possible during hostilities.[1]

The Alliance's general intentions are already spelled out if deterrence fails: to repel invaders immediately or contain them as near the Iron Curtain as possible.[2] It would be reasonable to assume that having done so the Alliance would prefer to come out of this initial defensive stage in a condition either to dictate a cease-fire and a Pact withdrawal, or to so dominate combat operations that subsequently the destruction of Pact forces in and approaching Western Europe can be threatened or accomplished. The detail to which their destruction would be necessary is a matter of conjecture. History shows that the man-by-man destruction of mass armies is difficult and often unnecessary. Certainly the French army of 1940 appeared powerful and resolute, yet it was beaten without decisively engaging most of its forces. Past experience indicates that early success plays a powerful role in force cohesion. Taking into account the motivation and nature of Pact forces, especially the non-Soviet ones, and the vulnerability of Soviet-type command systems and command styles to disruption and confusion, there is reason to hope that the destruction of the enemy might be accomplished by a stout defense against forces in contact, all the while cutting up his command chains, destroying his logistics, and causing dismay and doubt in his rear ranks. Just because of the sheer numbers of enemy forces, the allies should aim for France in 1940, not a Cannae or a Tannenberg.

This should not be taken to mean that the Alliance could conquer without bloodshed—far from it. But, if the allies can defend successfully long enough to frustrate the initial attack, then they may find, and probably would find, the Pact forces to their front more brittle than expected, and the field may well "open up" to the kind of maneuvering done best by armies that allow their subordinate leaders to be bold and to take the initiative.

Unfortunately, little has been said about reaching this point, even though there seems to be a reasonable chance that the initial attack could be contained. While war plans can never postulate in detail what actions should be taken during hostilities, NATO's strategy should attempt to shape a satisfactory conclusion as soon as possible after hostilities begin. Otherwise, it is left with what has been called an "open-ended war plan," scrambling after the Alliance is attacked to redefine goals, objectives, and war aims.[3] This is a legacy of the nullifying effect that deterrent theory has had on Western military strategy since 1947. In a review of NATO defense policy, Wolfgang Samuel has written:

> ... the alliance must address and define its warfighting goals over and above deterrence and the rapid employment of tactical nuclear weapons once deterrence has failed. Once conflict has joined, for whatever rational or irrational reason, what is the overall objective, and what are the immediate and intermediate goals of the Alliance? Failure of deterrence is considered so remote by some that it contributes to the acceptance of poorly-thought-through warfighting concepts ... the NATO goal then should be to reason before not after the unthinkable happens.[4]

SHAPING THE FIRST PHASES

After considering doctrine, forces, and a range of scenarios, an image begins to form of how a conventional conflict in central Europe might take shape. There probably would be a period of prehostilities buildup which, although neither side would be necessarily seeking war, would result in both sides preparing for it. (The causes are unimportant for this discussion.) At some point a Rubicon would be crossed in Western minds between political negotiations to deter conflict and the military preparation for it. The threshold is liable to be crossed unevenly, both horizontally—country by country—and vertically, possibly with those in lower echelons making the transition first, followed last by persons in the highest positions. It is not clear that Alliance members would wait for a NATO decision that hostilities were imminent. There are sufficient bilateral ties between the Big Four members—Britain, France, the United States, and West Germany—that most critical decisions could, and possibly would, take place outside the NATO framework. This period of prehostilities would be the *mobilization phase*, in which political efforts to dampen the crisis would continue, but the military emphasis on each side would be to gain, within political constraints, the most advantageous force posture possible in case negotiations should fail to defuse the situation.

Given Soviet military doctrine, it is reasonable to assume that hostilities would begin by an attack on the West by the Soviet Union and its allies. As has been pointed out, the Soviets then would be acting, in their eyes, entirely defensively, seeking to coopt NATO's attack options with a quick victory in order to terminate hostilities. The assault would open the *initial defense phase*.

Setting aside the question of ultimate Soviet political intentions, its battlefield objectives would be to split NATO, destroy U.S. nuclear weapons systems, and impose such a crushing defeat on Western forces that negotiation would appear to be a viable and welcome option for the Alliance. The first problem for the Alliance, therefore, is to repel and contain the Pact attack; the immediate problem of survival would make long-range issues academic. Assuming that nuclear weapons are not immediately used, the initial battle for the central front would last until the Soviets either had achieved their objectives and agreed to a cease-fire, or a cease-fire had been negotiated without either side achieving its goal (which generally would be a defeat for the Alliance since Pact troops would remain in West Germany), or with the exhaustion of committed Pact forces and a Soviet decision to continue the attack, perhaps at a slower tempo, and to await the arrival of the second strategic echelon to achieve breakthrough mass. The pacing factors are therefore the tempo of battle on the front, the progress of Pact forces, and the nuclear balance.

Assuming that NATO's front can hold, or at least frustrate, an immediate Pact breakthrough, a "window" opens that may offer NATO a breathing space between the commitment of first echelon forces in the initial attack and the arrival of Pact reinforcements. To use the word "opens" is perhaps misleading, as the beleaguered NATO forces holding the line would not be conscious of any letup. Indeed, committed Pact forces may well press even harder in an attempt to create favorable conditions that would open breakthrough opportunities and thus indicate more clearly a direction of movement for reinforcing units as they cross Poland and Czechoslovakia.

At the strategic level, however, there should be a window of uncertain duration, during which the committed first echelon Pact forces would have no reinforcements in depth. As has been discussed, the time required to close these units to the front depends on many variables. One 1980 Congressional Budget Office study has noted that, in this lull between the arrival of the first and second strategic echelons, the force ratio drops toward NATO's advantage.

In war gaming this scenario, the period between the arrival of the first and second strategic echelons consistently emerges as critical to the ultimate outcome of NATO's fortunes and initiates what could be called the *consolidation phase* of war: NATO has not collapsed, the breakthrough has not occurred, and SACEUR is now attempting to stabilize a defense and to look beyond the first shock. As the second echelon Soviet and Pact divisions are moving westward, American and other NATO reinforcements are arriving in Europe. For the most part, their disposition on arrival may be predetermined by short-term battlefield requirements. Some, however, may play a larger role in the battle beyond the second echelon.

The short-term objectives of SACEUR during this period, then, appear to be to survive the first attack and, in the period between the first and second frontal echelons, to build strength that can be used either to ride out the arrival of the second echelon, or to execute whatever other plans the Alliance requires. The important point is not what SACEUR does, but that the commander is able to use the gap between echelons to gain some freedom of action.

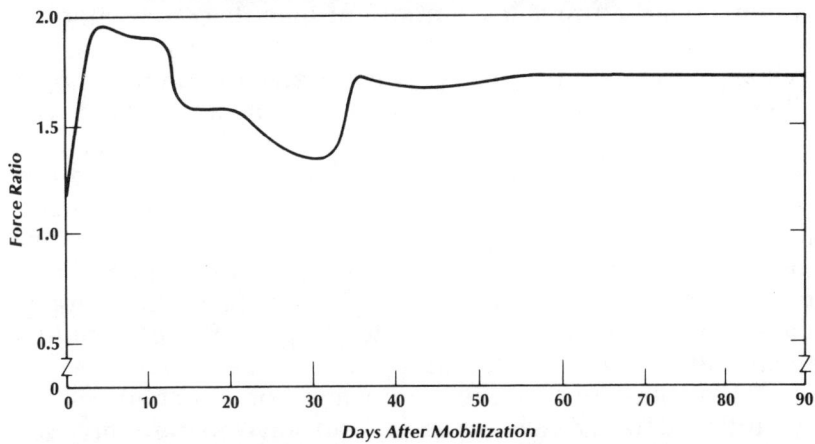

Shifting Warsaw Pact/NATO Force Balance in 1980: Ninety Days Following Pact Mobilization*

*This chart is illustrative only and does not reflect the more recent actions by the U.S. government and other NATO allies to upgrade mobilization or to assign more forces to NATO.
Source: Congressional Budget Office, *Army Ground Combat Modernization in the 1980s: Potential Costs and Effects for NATO* (Washington, DC: Government Printing Office, 1982), p. 29.

REACHING THE WINDOW

To ensure NATO's early survival and to put the Alliance in position to build strength, a sequence of decisions appears to be required soon after mobilization to open NATO's own windows of opportunity in the time continuum that marches toward D-day. None of the decisions requires NATO to commit to hostilities, and all are consistent with the Alliance's fundamentally defensive orientation. These actions broadly fall into mobilization activities and activities to build the SACEUR theater reserve.

FRANCE

France is obviously a key actor in any strategy of European conventional defense. Its sovereign foreign policy has made it strong, and its geography makes it vital. Although France withdrew from the NATO command structure in 1967, the issue always has been its relationship to NATO (and as a subset to the United States), not its position as a European member of the Alliance. Formal French reintegration into the NATO command structure is less important than its commitment to a forward role upon mobilization. A great deal of discrete military cooperation goes on today between France and its allies, and there is reason to assume that it would stand with the West in a crisis.[5] An agreement or understanding concerning the disposition of the French army should be sought by SACEUR early in the mobilization or prehostilities phase, if not sooner. In the largest sense, the exact nature of the disposition of French forces is not so important as that SACEUR be prepared—and be permitted—to free forces for employment in the NORTHAG area and to integrate France shoulder to shoulder in the Alliance defense.

Two conditions for the employment of French forces can be anticipated: French troops would have to be employed under national command, and they would have to be used in a manner that protected France directly.[6] Neither condition should preclude early and productive employment of the French since the sector currently occupied by the French Second Corps is behind the southern flank of Central Army Group (CENTAG), and that unit frequently participates in NATO exercises. Deployment of the French anywhere else but the southern half of CENTAG would not only violate the assumed requirement that French forces protect France but also would pose logistic problems of type (French forces use munitions peculiar to French equipment) and direction (French LOCs would cross those to U.S. and German units in the south).

Using the French only as a reserve for the southern flank of CENTAG, however, would be an inefficient use of the potentially second largest army in NATO and could lead to NATO battling for its life on the North German Plain, as untouched French units in the south supported forces that were not seriously threatened with breakthrough.[7] While the use of French forces as a southern reserve may be all that peacetime planning will countenance, the preferred course of action should be to open, as early as possible, a French national command along the German-Czech border in Bavaria and to relieve the armor-heavy German, and perhaps part of the U.S., corps in the sector (see Map 5).

The establishment of a French sector would emplace a French national command under CENTAG in the most advantageous location for France, directly shielding it with its own

Map 5. Recommended Corps Sectors in NATO

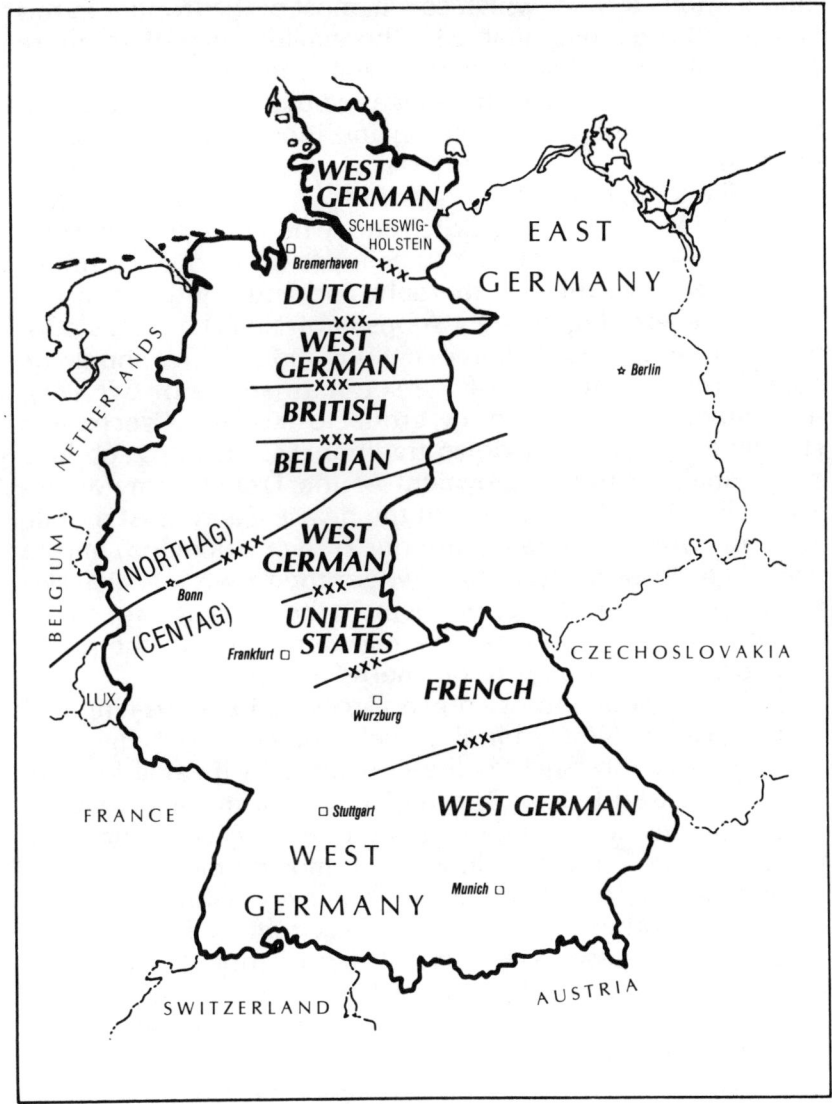

Source: Adapted from John M. Collins, *U.S.-Soviet Military Balance, 1960–1980* (Washington, DC: McGraw-Hill, 1980), p. 315. Reprinted by permission of John Collins and McGraw-Hill.

national forces and with the shortest LOCs possible. The mountainous terrain, which covers most of the frontier in this area, would be most suitable for the smaller and perhaps more agile French divisional structure, while the mobilized infantry units, as they arrived from France, would find themselves in terrain best suited for their organization and geographical location.

A French sector in Bavaria would place French, rather than German, forces opposing Czech and, when they arrived, Hungarian divisions. Too much can be made of national identities in Europe; nevertheless, the cohesion and fighting spirit of Pact armies are legitimately subjects of NATO strategy and, where possible, national predilections and enmities should be considered. In the case of the southern sector of CENTAG, movement of a French army group to face the Czechs and Hungarians would play down traditional German-Czech hostility. Finally, early employment of the French army allows SACEUR to withdraw several of the heaviest and most mobile divisions (some may remain under French command) and to shift them toward the center, where their own logistics systems can continue to support them. In the U.S. case, for example, this would mean maneuvering even closer to the ports, airfields, and stockpiles of northern Europe.

This introduction of French forces and the "freeing up" of a corps-plus element in Bavaria becomes a stepping-stone for further action, such as the creation of a theater reserve, to be discussed below. The difficulty of a massive relief in place and the involvement of such large forces cannot be underestimated, nor the difficulty of moving these huge formations rearward at a time when roads are liable to be congested with other military and civilian traffic. If history is a guide, the move should be possible if the proper logistic planning and traffic control measures have been taken. Certainly the history of Europe shows that large troop formations can be shifted laterally behind a line of contact. One future U.S. Army Chief of Staff made his reputation on such a move in 1918; in another war, the Third Army relieved Bastogne with a similar march. Once forces were relieved and moved rearward, the German road net would support north-south movement.

Unfortunately, the U.S. Army today has no experience in the movement of forces this large, and the officers who conducted the corps-sized armored movements of World War II have long been retired. But, if forces in the south cannot be shifted north and the French remain committed, by politics or logistics, to the south, then the opportunity would be lost to create a strong reserve in central or northern Europe, with unforeseeable consequences if the Pact achieved a breakthrough. If attempted, such a force substitution would be best executed at the earliest possible moment, preferably in the prehostilities period. If the initiative is not seized, forward units may be committed to the point that disengagement becomes impossible, and the French would have to be committed to combat piecemeal, if at all.

EAST-WEST LOCs

A second vital understanding between France and NATO involves the use of French ports and LOCs in an emergency. This kind of agreement can be "preloaded" prior to hostilities and can be negotiated on a low-key basis, thus easing any political strain within the Alliance, while sending a clear, yet nonaggressive, signal to the Pact.

NATO is extremely vulnerable logistically because of its dependence on Bremerhaven and the Low Country ports, which are open to attack from Eastern Europe, and from which stretches the long and easily interdicted U.S. supply line that runs parallel to the IGB and, in places, is practically within Soviet artillery range. In addition, allied aerial ports, through which would pass the early tip of the U.S. reinforcement flow, are all located well forward within range of Soviet tactical aircraft.

It would be vitally important, especially in a conventional war of uncertain duration, for NATO to employ protected ports and staging areas in which reinforcements and materiel can be received, sorted out, and sent forward. Again, all depends on timing. NATO's dependence on the northern ports puts its back to the wall on the northern flank immediately after hostilities. The very size of these ports makes their closure by conventional means difficult, although not impossible. But, as NATO forces are pushed back, as they likely would be in the initial stages, the ports would come under increasing attack by Pact air. Furthermore, the slender LOCs from the ports southward also would be vulnerable. Except in the most optimistic scenarios, it seems reasonable to assume that either NATO should seek deliberately to shift to more secure entry ports, or the decision may be forced upon it by the Pact.

It would then become desirable to consider two ramifications of shifting the LOCs, both of which are "war stoppers" if mismanaged. First would be the requirement to establish new supply facilities along the proposed LOCs within France, thereby involving the movement of substantial rolling stock, trucks, headquarters, and communications facilities across Europe, swinging from a north-south to an east-west orientation in a kind of grand logistics turning movement. Executing such a maneuver in peacetime would be difficult enough; to do it in war, with the constant demands that would continue to be placed on the facilities, would be exceedingly difficult. It becomes even more so without French cooperation and preplanning, especially in finding the manpower, communications facilities, traffic control agencies, and other resources that would have to come out of thin air, assuming that the German LOCs remained operational.

Shifting from the ports presently in use would involve a logistic campaign of the first magnitude. It is difficult to foresee how such a switch could be accomplished with less than about one month's advance planning. The redirection of shipping and arriving units, and the movement of transport to receive and deploy these units from their ports of entry, would require coordination and control on a global scope. Just the redirection of convoys or single ships, together with their naval protection, would be a huge undertaking. The decision to shift LOCs, in toto or in part, would be one of the truly significant decisions of the early phase of a crisis and would be unprecedented in scope and complexity. Even the allied shift from the beaches of Normandy to the captured ports in 1944 pales by comparison. French cooperation in this case is vital. The stockpiling of supplies to maintain the Alliance during the crossover period, or even the decision not to stockpile but to switch gradually, would have the greatest impact on the conduct of hostilities. The worst penalty for failure would be lost battles, with the next being lost opportunities, as a maneuver or offensive window might open and close for a SACEUR incapable of taking advantage of it.

For all these reasons, logistic discussions and preparations with France should begin almost with the first hint of a crisis involving NATO and the Pact. Discussing LOCs and supply need not be regarded as provocative or entangling; they are singularly defensive in nature. They are, however, vitally necessary.

MOBILIZATION

Mobilization within the Alliance may be executed in a number of ways and for a number of reasons. The critical factor is the political will and interests of each member state. Like the NATO alert, the decision to mobilize may not be taken first by the Alliance as a body but by individual countries as they become alarmed and act in their own self-interest. Once an alert begins, the various national forces will react to mobilization according to their own schedules and protocol. It is hoped that such a process would be orderly and in accordance with NATO procedures. It may well be uncoordinated, however, in the early stages until the NATO military command begins to sort things out.

As discussed in the partial mobilization scenario, mobilization, at least of the major central front powers, must begin no longer than seven days after the Soviets begin mobilizing. In a sense, then, the Soviets become the pacing factor for Western mobilization. It would seem that making this kind of linkage explicitly known to the Warsaw Pact would be a useful confidence-building or deterrent policy for NATO, rather than waiting for a crisis to inform the Soviets that the Alliance was mobilizing only in response to a similar Pact alert.

In addition to providing NATO the raw combat power that the Alliance needs in order to meet a Soviet-Warsaw Pact attack, mobilization could have a limited deterrent effect, in that it could be a signal that the mobilizing state views the situation seriously enough to bear the internal disruption caused by calling reservists to the colors. If that state quickly dominated the mobilization curve, and if the other side could be convinced that there would be no profit in further risk, the situation might be cooled down.

This raises the interesting possibility of using either reinforcement or mobilization, or a combination of both, as NATO deterrent measures during a prehostilities crisis. The idea must be approached cautiously. The historical precedent is for mobilization to be a provocation for similar moves by the opposition, and the ghost of 1914 hovers always in the background. But, while the West may fear reinforcement and mobilization, they remain indisputably necessary for any hope of a successful conventional defense. Further, U.S. mobilization and reinforcement of NATO, and concomitant peacetime planning and exercising, are tangible proofs of the U.S. commitment to its allies; hence, the political significance of the annual *Reforger* exercises. Given the extensive news coverage of even peacetime maneuvers, NATO reinforcement and mobilization in a crisis would take place in the full glare of the world's press and electronic media, which was not possible in 1914. Given that previous arrangements might have been made to explain U.S. countermoves categorically to the Pact, it should be possible for the United States to reassure its allies, signal determination to the prospective enemy, and still exercise restraint by sending over certain types of units, such as light infantry, rather than armored formations.

Making mobilization and deployment more viable tools for the civilian leadership would best be approached by mobilization systems designed to operate under positive control, for example, "packages" of units designed to deploy on order, independently of the main body of U.S. reinforcement and without drawing the main body of U.S. wide-bodied transport aircraft and fast shipping off balance. If political leaders can be freed of their justifiable fear of a coup by railroad timetable, mobilization thus can serve NATO in several dimensions.

For the United States, deployment to the theater is a complex problem quite different from that faced by the Dutch or the Danes. Rapid deployment of reinforcing packages to Europe virtually requires U.S. mobilization to some degree. The essence of the problem, if the president were to wish to initiate a limited reinforcement as a signal, would be to deploy limited forces without throwing off balance the plans and machinery required to begin massive reinforcement should the situation suddenly worsen. There are possibilities that, with POMCUS, some units of various types—light, armored, and mechanized—could be deployed almost entirely in commercial aircraft, either from the Civil Reserve Air Fleet or simply by charter airliners, either U.S. or NATO. The benefits gained would be that the U.S. Air Force's fleet of wide-bodied cargo carriers would be generally untouched and could remain cocked for heavier duties should the situation demand it. Since the president currently can mobilize a limited number of reservists on his own authority, the beginning of the deployment "flow" can start relatively quickly and then be followed by appropriate legislation. The U.S. Department of Defense is in the process of overhauling its mobilization system.[8]

LIGHT FORCES

POMCUS units capable of moving rapidly and drawing prepositioned equipment in Europe already have been discussed. Additionally, the U.S. Army is in the process of establishing a number of light divisions in its regular army structure. Although the units have been designed primarily for deployment to underdeveloped areas of the world, they also will be available for deployment to Europe. According to Drew Middleton, "in the event of a war in Europe, the division would not try to engage armored forces but would deploy in forests or urban areas, or what the planners call 'closed terrain.' The planners are giving attention to tactics for combat in urban areas in West Germany and elsewhere."[9] Middleton also has noted that these divisions would utilize from 400 to 500 sorties of C-141Bs, the air force's standard transport. Deployment of these kinds of units, along with the POMCUS armored divisions, would raise the number of flags in Europe early in the reinforcement phase.

The implications to U.S. and NATO strategy of light, purely defensive units deployed early to the European theater in a crisis have not yet been fully explored. From the point of view of prehostilities utility, in the period when Western and Pact leaders would be attempting concurrently to send nonaggressive signals and still prepare for the worst, light forces, by their nature, would seem to be nonthreatening to the Pact's leadership. In the U.S. case, their light organization should permit their deployment in civilian air transports, either in the Civil Reserve Air Fleet, or, at a lower level of reaction, in commercial charters. The bulk of the air force's heavy lift fleet would then not be committed prematurely, which has both political and military advantages.

With U.S. light divisions, initial planning indicates that

they are austerely designed, with artillery and support units "plugged" into them as appropriate for the mission.[10] Of the two likely areas where light forces could be employed defensively in Europe, one is in CENTAG in the mountainous terrain already in a U.S. corps sector but which possibly would be taken over by a French command. The second is in the densely urbanized North German Plain around Hannover where the Belgian and British corps are stationed.

In terms of political reassurance for NATO as well as military dispositions, it would seem advantageous if the U.S. divisions could be deployed into the northern urban areas, perhaps under the operational control of British I Corps, where their early arrival in this critical sector would be a statement of U.S. support of the Alliance and where their deployment, logistic, and fire support could be provided by the British, perhaps with some prestocking assistance from the United States.[11]

Finally, if light forces were to be deployed in sufficient time to take up defensive positions immediately behind forward-deployed armored or mobile units now stationed in Europe, some armored formations could be withdrawn from the IGB. The movement of selected armored units away from the border would be a useful political signal of nonaggressive intent, would materially reduce the chance of accidental conflict, and could be beneficial in terms of public reassurance. However, it also would give NATO a chance in the prehostilities phase to constitute the maximum number of armored reserves and, as such, would be a military signal to the Pact which would be hard to ignore. To the Soviets, it would affect the central front correlation of forces by building the kind of NATO defense with which Soviet doctrine is least able to cope.

The battlefield utility of light forces in central Europe has been debated, and exaggerated, on all sides. The arguments for defenses in depth manned by light infantry armed with antitank weapons overlook the fact that NATO, and West Germany in particular, have not much depth to give.[12] If they are employed forward, light forces should expect to be employed in fixed defenses in roughly linear fashion, intermingled with heavy armored or mechanized formations, from which they will gain fire support and some form of tactical mobility. This is not to say that light forces alone could stand up to armored attack; they could not. In many sectors only armored formations have the mobility and firepower to confront other armor head-on, almost regardless of preparation time. In some areas, however, light forces could play an indirectly conclusive role to reinforce critical points and to relieve armored units for the decisive war of maneuver. On the central front, if NATO's objective is to survive and eventually prevail, the Alliance must ultimately have strong, highly mobile, and heavily gunned armored forces capable of defeating Soviet tanks on their own terms and wresting the initiative from the Soviets.

At present, the deployment of NATO's armored forces is forward, which is well suited for countering a surprise or short-notice attack when meeting engagements and hastily prepared obstacles would put a premium on mobility and firepower, and when the probability of a protracted war is likely to be low. In a mobilization scenario, since expensive NATO armored formations are unlikely ever to be as numerous as Pact forces, a conventional defense strategy in this kind of situation should consider husbanding, as far as is practical, potentially decisive armored and mechanized divisions for counterattacks in the initial phases, and possibly offensive operations at a later time. The opportunity that light forces offer, in selected areas, to pull some armored units into reserve should not be wasted.

With time to prepare obstacles, deployment and fortification of light forces, armed with antitank weapons in economy-of-force missions to "thicken up" defenses in certain areas, make good military sense. Robert Komer has noted that "the increasing urban sprawl in the Center Region (plus the fact that 40 per cent of Germany is forested) creates a situation in which 'straight leg infantry' units well equipped with antiarmor weapons could be highly useful."[13] Further, deployed light forces consume less logistic fodder than heavy forces and thus could be supported with fewer resources and less congestion, a real advantage for logistics-starved commanders.[14] The U.S. concept of support plugs should provide almost an ideal interface with NATO common item support systems.

If light forces are available in sufficient quantity, and the decision is made to employ them in an economy-of-force role, their emplacement behind barriers and in suitable terrain is best accomplished in the prehostilities phase, either behind forward-deployed units, or, if the terrain were especially favorable, forward. If no disposition were made until after the start of hostilities, the opportunity to get the maximum utility from emplacement, fortifications, and barriers would be lost.

The second role for light forces is no less vital: to provide rear security behind the line of contact against Soviet airborne and helicopter-borne troops. Given present force levels and doctrine, forward divisions would find it difficult to divert subordinate units to secure their own rear areas, let alone those belonging to higher headquarters.[15] The West German Territorial Army has been assigned rear-area security as its primary mission, one in which its home-guard regiments would be supplemented by various other smaller security units and local police.[16]

A disadvantage that light forces may encounter in the rear-area security role would be a lack of tactical and operational mobility caused by the nature of their organization and exacerbated by the requirement to react quickly to penetrating forces before they solidified gains. Some tactical mobility assets could probably be constituted by local means. The security role would be doubly difficult because of the large numbers of civilian refugees and the requirement for refugee control, which is a national responsibility but which will divert national assets from security missions. The impact of civilian refugees on military operations could be considerable, especially in terms of preventing the movement of tactical and operational reserve and security forces. Air mobility might well find its greatest use in a European scenario to be that of lifting battalion- or brigade-sized reaction forces over the heads of civilian refugee traffic and military units in order to strike quickly at Soviet attempts to penetrate and disrupt rear-area operations.

BARRIERS

In the densely urbanized areas along the IGB, and in particular where the Soviet main attack most probably would fall, extensive urbanization provides opportunities for constructing obstacles in depth which could disrupt advancing Soviet forces. Used in conjunction with fortified defenses, barriers could significantly enhance the economy-of-force mission of light and home-guard type forces.

Construction and use of barriers have long been advocated by many Western strategists, and their potential utility is unquestioned. They would force the attacker to concentrate his forces more heavily, break the momentum of the attack, and allow NATO to hold more ground with fewer resources.[17] Ideally, barriers should be constructed well ahead of hostilities, even in peacetime.

Aside from funding, there are political problems that make this scenario a remote possibility. In time of tension, authorization for construction of barriers probably would have a great symbolic effect, in the political sense, as the crossover point from deterrence measures to preparations for war. For this reason, and because of the inevitable physical damage that would occur to private property, construction of barriers likely would be delayed until the last minute, necessitating their construction in some areas behind forward-deployed forces. West Germany's considerable construction industry, already incorporated into its defense planning, should be able to provide a substantial capability for building antitank ditches, abatis, minefields, weapons emplacements, and other fortifications.

NAVAL FORCES

The disposition of naval forces in the prehostilities phase is crucially important. Fortunately, the movement of battle groups is less provocative than the mobilization and deployment of ground and air forces.

Of critical importance to NATO's naval strategy is the situation regarding the four Soviet fleets—Northern, Baltic, Black, and Pacific—and their SSBNs and attack submarines. In any case involving the risk of war between the Soviet Union and the United States, the proper course for U.S. naval strategy is to be positioned to render the Soviets ineffective at sea. This can best be done, if there is a prehostilities phase, by guarding those strategic areas through which the Soviets must pass to gain the open ocean. In particular, those areas are the Greenland-Iceland-United Kingdom (G-I-UK) Gap in the North Atlantic, the neck of the Baltic, the eastern Mediterranean, and the exits to the Sea of Okhotsk and the port of Petropavlovsk in the Pacific. Of these, the most vital and most difficult, save perhaps for the Okhotsk exits, is the G-I-UK Gap. Soviet submarines flushed from their bases in Murmansk and

Archangel, if allowed to break into the open ocean, could dangerously affect the NATO Atlantic SLOCs. If naval forces were prepositioned in time, escaping submarines could be detected and followed.

The whole subject of the northern flank, as seen in the context of prehostility maneuvering, becomes an area of special interest. While both sides may have great reluctance to provoke hostilities on the central front, more risks may be taken in the isolated North Atlantic. This is especially true in northern Norway, whose tip juts down into the core of NATO's defense area, and from whose air bases the G-I-UK Gap can be dominated by air power. The nature of Norway's geographical isolation from central Europe, combined with its strategically vital location in relation to the northern naval campaign and its potential for air attacks through NATO's "back door," should lead to early NATO action to reinforce Norwegian defenses with the U.S. Marine brigade currently scheduled, plus reinforcements from Britain and Canada.

NATO's southern flank should be less insecure. The presence of two strong NATO partners in Greece and Turkey, in addition to the relatively lower Warsaw Pact threat, should allow NATO commanders in the area some breathing room. Indeed, NATO planners may well regard, with some appreciation, the comparatively lightly defended southern route to the interior of the Soviet Union. Certainly there will be a strong interest in bottling up the Black Sea Fleet.

It is historical fact—one that is rediscovered when thinking about extended conventional defense in Europe—that once hostilities begin the military and political utility of naval forces increases with the duration of the conflict. Therefore, although U.S. and NATO naval forces initially would play a relatively minor direct role in a central front battle, their potential direct effect increases as time passes. This is partly because of the indirect effect that sea power has traditionally played, such as in security SLOCs, and partly because modern weaponry offers peripheral operations more direct effect on inland Europe.

THE SACEUR RESERVE

On the sixth day after he became prime minister of Great Britain, Winston Churchill attended a May 1940 meeting in Paris. German armies were pouring into France, the French army was everywhere falling back, communications were disrupted, and the atmosphere was one of gloom and defeat. The French commander in chief briefed from a map:

> When he stopped there was considerable silence. I then asked 'Where is the strategic reserve?' . . . General Gamelin turned to me and, with a shake of the head and a shrug, said 'Aucune [None].'
> There was another long pause. . . . I was dumbfounded. . . . It had never occurred to me that any commanders having to defend five hundred miles of engaged front would have left themselves unprovided with a mass of maneuver. No one can defend with certainty so wide a front; but when the enemy has committed himself to a major thrust which breaks the line, one can always have, one *must* always have, a mass of divisions which marches up in vehement counter-attack at the moment when the first fury of the offensive has spent its force.[18]

Of the many hazards inherent in defending NATO's eastern border with too few forces, the most serious is the lack of strategic and theater reserves to counter possible Soviet breakthroughs, or to threaten offensive action to seize the initiative once the initial attack has been contained. Short of containment, no task will be more important in the early stages of conflict than the constitution of strong reserves, both on the Continent (under AFCENT) at the theater level, and, on the strategic level, under SACEUR for NATO overall.

The inadequacy of NATO's operational reserves has been noted and commented upon in many studies, usually in the context of pointing out the need for additional NATO forces. "The real problem has been the conspicuous lack of operational reserves," writes Peter Stratmann. "There is a growing tendency to ignore this simple fact and to invoke—in the best traditions of bourgeois idealism—the importance of 'innovative doctrine,' which is, of course, much easier than to pay for additional divisions needed."[19] Another analyst, Steven Canby, has long argued that a lack of operational reserves is NATO's gravest conventional deficiency. The U.S. Department of Defense, in its 1981 annual report, said essentially the same thing. But identifying the issue has not solved the immediate problem. While in the future it may be possible for enough forces to be raised to provide adequate theater and strategic reserves, the immediate problem is to plan for their creation out of resources already at hand, or that will be at hand by 1986.

All combat units attempt to maintain reserves by which a commander can influence the course of battle by forces under his control. Usually the commitment of the reserve is the last throw before *decisive commitment*, a point at which no maneuver is possible and all forces are fighting.

Going back to the distinctions between tactical, operational, and strategic levels, the term "operational reserve" refers here to brigade or divisional formations withheld at the corps or Army Group level, such as CENTAG or NORTHAG, with which to influence the battle in their sector. Closer to the front, commanders at lower levels would doubtless attempt to maintain a tactical reserve of some type, although the sheer numbers of a likely Pact attack would limit the size of formations that could be held back. The U.S. Army's operational doctrine concerning the size of reserve formations states that in defense "commanders down to brigade will normally try to retain about one-third of their maneuver strength in reserve."[20] One-third back is also about the proportion of Warsaw Pact forces in the second echelon, which in an attack would perform essentially a reserve mission.

In NATO at present, however, the size of the operational reserves appears to be significantly less than the Pact's forces: a division for each Army Group, a brigade for a corps, and so on, roughly one-sixth of deployed strength.[21] Given the paucity of NATO forces and the severity of an expected attack, it may be difficult for commanders in threatened sectors to withhold even that small amount. The relatively modest size of all reserves indicates that, with the possible exception of holding back some of the POMCUS-based U.S. divisions, there would be few forces at any level below AFCENT which would be able to deal effectively with one or more Pact breakthroughs, especially if the Soviets employed Operational Maneuver Group-type operations once they succeeded in penetrating NATO's forward defense.[22] This might be acute if reserves were so thinly spread that they would have to be moved any distance to be employed. The probability is high that, in the initial stages and in spite of the efforts of the West German Territorials, road nets are liable to be congested and movement difficult near the line of contact. At the theater level, Com-AFCENT may be strongly tempted to use early arriving divisions to reinforce and back up his hard-pressed forward forces, themselves short of reserves. In doing so, Peter would be robbed to pay Paul. Sending forces forward immediately might be necessary to avert immediate disaster, but it also would severely restrict AFCENT's ability to influence the later battle. In military terms, AFCENT is decisively engaged soon after hostilities begin. On the theater level, therefore, ComAFCENT needs operational reserves in order first to ensure his defense and second to take advantage of whatever operational opportunities he can wrest within his theater.

On the strategic level, SACEUR, who must oversee the entire NATO war from the northern flank to the southern border of Turkey, lacks even a deployable corps with which to influence the balance, a requirement that is key to envisioning and planning the course of the conflict beyond the initial stages. With no way for SACEUR to shape subsequent phases—for NATO to take the initiative—NATO's only option, short of capitulation or nuclear use, is to soak up the Warsaw Pact attack, averting disaster but slowly losing ground until either a cease-fire can be negotiated, or the arrival of the full second strategic echelon increases the odds against the West and probably escalates the war to the nuclear threshold. With SACEUR reserves, however, NATO's conventional options increase to three: negotiate from a cease-fire line somewhere within the Federal Republic, counterattack on the central front and attempt to push back the advancing Pact forces, or try to gain some kind of advantage by indirect attacks that will force the Soviets and their allies to divert from their main effort, destroy their forces, weaken their alliance, and lead to negotiations.[23] (Negotiation by NATO from a cease-fire line within the Federal Republic, without a clear military advantage on the battlefield, makes returning to the status quo ante bellum very unlikely. It therefore should be discarded.[24])

A central front counterattack presupposes a long-term logistic buildup and the risk of a war of attrition that would destroy central Europe. Providing AFCENT with sufficient theater reserves would tend to drive the conflict in this direction even if the forces provided are sufficiently mobile to avoid "meat grinder" attritional battles. However mobile and skillfully led, though, their potential for a decisive and early conventional decision is liable to be questionable. Once battle is joined on the central front, the West's ability to achieve a clear advantage *within theater* may take, in the best case, agonizing weeks or months. While a nonnuclear war in Europe in which neither side achieves an early victory is better than an early loss, NATO's emphasis in a conventional war plan should be victory as defined in the objectives of flexible response.[25] To plan otherwise for a war of attrition is politically infeasible and militarily inexcusable.

The third option—gaining an advantage indirectly—is only possible with a SACEUR reserve of sufficient mobility to seize quickly opportunities in Pact dispositions during the war's early stages, probably within the first sixty days. If strong mobile forces were to be available in sufficient quantity, they could take advantage of NATO's possession of the rim around the Soviet empire, probable Pact weaknesses on the flanks of the main theaters, move quickly to force the enemy to begin responding to NATO initiatives, and allow SACEUR the chance to dictate his own strategic tempo and terms. There are potential targets; since the Pact must concentrate for the decisive blow, SACEUR's dispositions in other areas would leave certain vital areas uncovered. Reinforcement of Denmark might be a mission of some urgency, following which a mobile force poised in Denmark would look southeast at enfilading the Pact forces in central Europe. At a very minimum, the capability to execute such a theater deployment would pose a sufficient threat to the Pact that second strategic echelon forces heading toward the battlefield would have to be diverted from likely breakthrough sectors on the North German Plain to secure probable allied objectives. In other words, the Soviets would have to concern themselves with SACEUR's conventional options, which is not the case today.

This option bears a superficial resemblance to the idea of "horizontal escalation," a concept for global strategy that is flawed by the inability of indirect pressure outside NATO to effect decisively the central front battle. The difference is that in this case, the SACEUR reserve would be used directly against the center or the flanks of the central front itself in order to disrupt Soviet plans bearing directly on the battlefield. In addition, the use of a powerful reserve force somewhere on the rim or in central Europe could enhance an AFCENT offensive, even a limited one, if the opportunity were presented.

There is another caution in considering this concept. No military planner or civilian policymaker should be deceived into thinking that a maneuver strategy alone could be conclusive without operational and tactical battle at the decisive points. The objective of a theater-level maneuvering force should be to assist or make possible the destruction of the Warsaw Pact armies in central Europe by employing heavy mobile forces organized along the lines envisioned for 1985–86. As their offensive falters, the General Staff of the Soviet armed forces must be forced to address not only the resumption of its offensive but also threats from fresh NATO forces, both within theater and without, that directly challenge Soviet and Pact forces in Europe. The key, then, is frustration of the initial Soviet attack and, by the time their follow-on armies are in the process of a difficult movement toward the front, the rapid multiplication of nonnuclear threats to Soviet forces. Rapidity must be stressed; the Soviets know, as does NATO, that the USSR can least afford a long war. Thus the essence of the NATO plan must be to defend, regroup, and defeat Soviet forces quickly, as well as to make the Kremlin face the nuclear decision early when it still has the option of negotiating an end to hostilities without facing total defeat. A drawn-out war, from the Soviets' viewpoint, would place them at sufficient risk anyway so as to make a nuclear strike more attractive.

Planning for the use of a true SACEUR strategic reserve involves a reorientation from short war to indefinite war perspectives. The use of a strategic reserve at this level is a complicated process. Time is a dimension of the reserve that becomes more critical at higher and higher echelons of operation. The movement and employment of tactical reserves can be measured in minutes and hours; at the operational level, in days. At the strategic level, days and weeks would be required to mount a significant attack of the kind that would force the Soviets to react.

This type of lead time for planning requires thinking about a war of several campaigns in Europe and would necessitate strategic planning to be going forward on many levels even as the initial Pact attack is being absorbed on the central front. Without doing so, however, NATO is liable to arrive at the "window of opportunity," created by Soviet mobilization and delay of the second strategic echelon, only to have no options other than to continue receiving the Soviet attack.

To give SACEUR that kind of flexibility, his reserve force would have to meet three requirements. First, it should be a formidable fighting force, one that is mobile, self-contained, and logistically supportable. Second, it should be composed of forces already existing, or planned to exist, by 1986. Third, it should be constituted within SACEUR's area but far enough back that it is secure from theater-level attack and reconnaissance. Therefore, reserves should be made available at two levels: a theater reserve for AFCENT and a strategic reserve for SACEUR, the former functioning more in a classic reserve role, the second to give SACEUR the leverage to take advantage of opportunities for regaining the initiative within the first sixty days of war.

In a surprise attack scenario there would be no opportunity for AFCENT to constitute a reserve, but neither would there be one for the attacking force. In the partially mobilized scenario, however, if the French come in prior to D-day, the establishment of a French field army sector would provide the opportunity for AFCENT to withdraw substantial forces in the south and to shift them to the vital center. The nature of the operations involved, from logistic stockpiling to handing over communications facilities, sectors of responsibility, and actually exchanging units, would all require a significant amount of preplanning, which in the partially mobilized scenario would imply decisions made and planning begun even prior to M-day. Barrier construction, reinforcement by light forces, and other mobilization measures also would require coordination but would not hinder the turnover.

The establishment of a SACEUR strategic reserve poses a more complex problem. The force should be assembled far enough removed from the theater of operations to be generally secure and yet be centrally located and close enough that it could be quickly moved within the theater and logistically supported without diverting air and sealift devoted to the central front. Northern Britain seems ideal, although perhaps there are other locations as well. Planning for retention of mechanized or armored forces seems impractical because of the urgent need for those kinds of forces on the central front and the requirement for rapid mobility throughout the NATO theater. In the case of the United States, the most strategically mobile army units currently in the force structure, and scheduled to be there in 1985–86, are an airborne division and an air assault division, both of which also may be dedicated to the central front as light infantry, with the exception of their antiarmor helicopters but with subsequent loss of their strategic mobility capability. There is also an Airborne Corps headquarters, complete with the attendant communications, medical, and other kinds of support needed by frontline divisions. The corps headquarters would offer excellent planning and execution of the reserve mission.

In the case of the air assault division, its light combat units and helicopters are designed to be quickly air-loaded and deployed. On arrival in a combat zone, it would have considerable combat mobility and antiarmor capability in its armed helicopters as long as they did not operate directly against first echelon air defenses. In a different role, divisional light combat units could rapidly self-deploy from Britain across the Channel to counter threats within AFCENT. This is particularly valuable when considering the need for quick mobile forces in the theater role to counter Soviet air-landed forces in NATO's rear areas. For this reason perhaps the air assault formations would have a theater "string" attached.

The airborne division likewise could deploy as light infantry. It has the advantage of being capable of seizing its own airheads without landing aircraft, but the complexity of mounting large parachute operations virtually demands that this capability be controlled at the SACEUR level, at least initially. From SACEUR's perspective, airborne forces have the advantage of being able to move quickly anywhere in his theater in transport aircraft not generally required for strategic lift. Once on the ground, however, they suffer the same vulnerabilities as do all light forces in contact with armor: they must be sited in suitable terrain and be supported by air. Both the air assault and airborne formations are decisively engaged once they come into contact with armored units because they lack the mobility to maneuver.

The air assault and airborne divisions available in the U.S. force structure are also dedicated to contingencies in the Persian Gulf region as part of the U.S. Rapid Deployment Force.[26] It is erroneous, however, to assume, as some analysts do, that these forces would not be available to SACEUR should war break out in Europe.[27] The availability of these light forces depends on which theater has priority or is activated first. If these two divisions already are deployed elsewhere when hostilities begin on the Continent, there are other NATO forces with similar capabilities available that could be assigned a SACEUR reserve role, such as German, British, or French parachute or light infantry units. Elements of the French Rapid Action Force would be very useful in this role.[28]

Ultimately, if the creation of a SACEUR mobile reserve were needed, the Rapid Deployment Force requirement could be passed to other light formations in order to maintain a strategic forced-entry capability for the most serious contingency. The recent trend in the U.S. Army toward raising new light divisions, as well as reconfiguring existing forces, makes forces available for this kind of mission.

A third useful force for the SACEUR reserve role would be a U.S. MAB, if one could be made available. A MAB offers the advantage of sea mobility, provided its amphibious lift remains attached, and its own air support. Its ground elements also can be task-organized to move by airland. Depending on its task organization, a MAB's air support can vary from helicopters to FA-18s, with vertical takeoff AV-8Bs in the middle of the spectrum. In addition, it has some armor and lightweight antiarmor vehicles, although it remains primarily light infantry. Assignment of a MAB to the SACEUR reserve role would allow NATO to capitalize on its expected superiority at sea, a superiority that grows more important to NATO as the duration of hostilities increases, although the force could be employed with army elements anywhere tactical air transport can land, as well as by sea.

Where a MAB would come from would depend on the disposition of the three divisions of marines at the beginning of hostilities; perhaps more critically, on the disposition of amphibious assault shipping. Even with a division-plus commitment to the Persian Gulf and a brigade commitment to Norway, sufficient marine forces and lift should remain for use by SACEUR in the most critical sector. On a long-term basis, there have been proposals that Canada shift its NATO commitment north from southern Germany. In fact, it is scheduled to reinforce Norway with a brigade group deployed from Canada. Although the actual plans seem doubtful at present, there is evidently reawakened interest in Canada in bolstering its national contribution to NATO.[29] A way to speed up the process might be for the Canadians to purchase the U.S. equipment prepositioned there and to assume the mission earmarked for the marines, thus freeing a MAB for the reserve role.

Deployment of forces for the SACEUR reserve should be possible without disrupting the movement of urgently needed forces to the central region. The marine brigade could move on its own amphibious lift from wherever it is when mobilization begins, requiring only the additional escort protection necessary to transit. Deployment of its air component would require in-air refueling, but the tanker support needed could come from the marines' own propjet C-130 tankers, which are not suitable aircraft for support of faster C-141 strategic lift missions or B-52s. Movement of the airborne division and airmobile division from the United States could be delayed until the SLOC is firmly established to the central region, and then the two units could be moved either by sea or by air since, after the SLOC closes, most unit movement takes place by sea, leaving some relative slack in the air bridge. The essential point here is not the particulars of how such a force could be constituted and deployed but to raise the possibility that there could be such a force at all, to examine the manner in which it might influence a conventional battle in the hazy distance beyond the initial defense of Europe, and then to work backward to weigh the costs and benefits of its constitution.

Notes

[1] Immersion in detail is unavoidable in war planning. Although wars are directed from the top, they are fought and decided from the ground up, and possible battlefield outcomes must be carefully and objectively calculated to provide a realistic basis for estimates. Such scenarios are also necessary for force planners to rationalize and develop requirements. Thus a detailed examination must be made of possible Soviet-Warsaw Pact attacks on the Alliance in order to examine, for instance, the adequacy of rear-area security forces or of NATO's tank-truck capacity. Such requirement plans should not be confused with the real McCoy: to plan for the actual employment of existing forces. Unfortunately, force planning sometimes does intrude.

[2] John M. Collins, *Grand Strategy* (Annapolis, MD: Naval Institute Press, 1973), pp. 132–34.

[3] Ikle, *Every War Must End*, pp. 2–8.

[4] Wolfgang W. E. Samuel, "The Impossible Task—Defense Without Relevant Strategy," *Air University Review*, 31, no. 3 (March–April 1980): 22–23.

[5] Robert W. Komer, "Is Conventional Defense of Europe Feasible?" *Naval War College Review* 35, no. 5 (September–October 1982): 84; Berger, "The Course of French Defense Policy," p. 25.

[6] Steven T. Ross, "French Defense Policy," *Naval War College Review* 36, no. 3 (May–June 1983): 35.

[7] The French government is considering, however, development of a new French corps designed for commitment anywhere on the central front, rather than exclusively in southern Germany. Ibid., p. 33.

[8] *DoD 1984 Budget*, pp. 261–68.

[9] Drew Middleton, "For U.S. Army, A New Kind of Infantry Division," *New York Times*, 19 February 1984.

[10] Deputy Chief of Staff for Operations, *The U.S. Army Light Infantry Division* (Washington, DC: Department of the Army, 1984), p. 13.

[11] Such an arrangement also would lend itself to less expensive and politically advantageous deployment exercises in peacetime to complement the annual *Reforger* maneuvers.

[12] See Robert W. Komer, "Treating NATO's Self-Inflicted Wound," *Foreign Policy* 13 (Winter 1973–74): 34–48. See also Steven L. Canby, "Dampening Nuclear Counterforce Incentives: Correcting NATO's Inferiority in Conventional Military Strength," *Orbis* 19, no. 1 (Spring 1975): 66.

[13] Komer, "Is Conventional Defense of Europe Feasible?" p. 83.

[14] Robert B. Killebrew, "Has Light Infantry *Really* Had Its Day?" *Army* 29, no. 12 (December 1979): 47.

[15] John B. Reisz, "Rear Area Combat Operations," *Military Review* 50, no. 12 (December 1979): 62.

[16] *1983 White Paper*, p. 154.

[17] Kaufmann, "Nuclear Deterrence in Central Europe," in Steinbruner and Segal, *Alliance Security*, pp. 65–71.

[18] Winston S. Churchill, *Their Finest Hour* (Boston: Houghton Mifflin, 1949), p. 47.

[19] Stratmann, "Prospective Tasks and Capabilities," p. 163.

[20] *Operations* (1982), p. 11–8.

[21] Mako, *U.S. Ground Forces*, p. 37.

[22] Mearsheimer, "Why the Soviets Can't Win Quickly in Central Europe," p. 23.

[23] Samuel Huntington has proposed a NATO offensive strategy that would plan for a counteroffensive into Eastern Europe as a conventional deterrent strategy. (Huntington, *The Strategic Imperative* [Cambridge, MA: Ballinger, 1982]). While there are numerous arguments against his proposal, Huntington is at least attempting to answer the questions about conventional strategy.

[24] Indeed, this would be an advantageous position for the Pact. A cease-fire on West German territory is the alternative currently facing NATO strategic thinking, and this leaves the Pact—the Soviets—in possession of the ground. In this case, it could be expected that Soviet political objectives become to stop the fighting as quickly as possible and to negotiate some form of a neutralized central Europe.

[25] Collins, *Grand Strategy*, pp. 132–34.

[26] *DoD 1984 Budget*, p. 195.

[27] Mako, in *U.S. Ground Forces*, p. 133, makes such an assumption.

[28] The German parachute brigades have other missions but could be reoriented. Use of the French Rapid Action Force would have to be negotiated as circumstances permitted. Even allowing the priority for Southwest Asia, American light forces are the first choice because they are most liable to be available. *Military Balance, 1983–1984*, p. 34.

[29] Nils Ørvik, "A Defence Doctrine for Canada," *Orbis* 27, no. 1 (Spring 1983): 201.

Chapter Six

Finding the Right Questions

THE DIFFICULTIES of coming to grips with NATO conventional defense within the existing framework of political and military realities should be evident. Aside from the purely military questions of resources, operations, and assets, three larger questions emerge.

NATO SENSITIVITY

First is NATO's political sensitivity to any apparent weakening of nuclear deterrence, especially if an American source is boosting nonnuclear defense. The point has to be made plainly that nuclear weapons are now a permanent part of the defense plans of all countries. They are never going to go away, and NATO and the West will continue to need modern, effective nuclear forces for the foreseeable future. A conventional warfighting strategy for NATO does not lessen the Alliance's dependence on nuclear deterrence; it merely responds to changing strategic conditions. A strong conventional defense enhances deterrence by withholding from the Soviets the option of a nonnuclear win and forces them, rather than the West, to confront the nuclear decision. In other words, the Soviet Union's crisis options would be closed out before they could launch a defensive preemptive attack on NATO. They could not win conventionally, nor could they win with conventional forces and nuclear weapons together. In the long term, the most satisfactory result of a confident defense may be that the Soviet Union will modify its military doctrine of blitzkrieg preemption, which is the preeminent hazard in Europe today. Given the ability of the Soviet leadership to control the military's bias for tanks and offensive combat attack aircraft, a defensive posture in Eastern Europe would serve the Soviet Union well.[1]

THREAT CONSENSUS

Second is the difficulty of arriving at a consensus on the nature of the threat. There is an urgent need for a NATO agreement on the dimensions of the Soviet threat to Western Europe, against which Alliance members may posture forces. This agreement should address such vital issues as the scenario against which NATO would place its first priority, a uniform estimate of Soviet mobilization capabilities, and an agreement, among other things, on allied mobilization responses and times. Without agreement, each member draws its own conclusions and builds its own forces. The lack of consensus is especially galling in conventional defense. In mitigation of NATO's difficulties, threat assessments at the political level are fraught with pitfalls affecting national economies, internal politics, and issues that, to the soldier, deal only on the periphery of the central issues but are life and death to elected leaders.

As a minimum, however, there should be agreement on the most likely form of Soviet attack (understanding that any attack is unlikely so long as an effective Western defense is maintained), then the next most likely, then the next, and so on. Only in this way can the Alliance decide how to match its forces against requirements and decide what risks it is willing to take in certain areas. Covering all the bases equally will be prohibitively expensive and is probably beyond NATO's reach. Some bases can be covered less than others.

This study submits that the most likely threat scenario would reflect both sides partially mobilized and a general balance in tactical and theater nuclear weapons. The bolt-from-the-blue scenario, although possible, has been discarded because of operational difficulties and political infeasibility. Likewise, a scenario in which both sides were fully mobilized has been dropped. In such a case, the Soviets appear to be at a disadvantage; they either would probably not attack west or they would immediately use nuclear weapons. Neither the surprise attack nor the full mobilization attack is impossible, but the partial mobilization scenario seems to be more credible in terms of possible Western and Pact reactions and capabilities.

BUILDING A BOX

Third is the difficulty of "building a box," or of defining the objectives and restraints, of a strategy of conventional defense for NATO. Western military and civilian strategic analysts have concentrated long on the conditions that might occur prior to war, or in the very early stages of a Soviet or Pact attack. Less has been written about the conditions that could be expected after the first fifteen days, thirty days, or beyond. Not much has been written at all about how the Alliance would want to stop a war with the Soviet Union, other than to say, as NATO does, that NATO's territory should be restored. But what, for example, of the Soviet or Pact forces that might be on allied territory? Assuming that NATO forces conducted a successful defense after initial losses, should the allies negotiate from an in-place halt, or seek the destruction and forcible eviction of Pact forces before any cease-fire?

These kinds of questions, and others, are implicit in thinking about a conventional defense posture that has a logical end. They must be addressed in peacetime because they drive premobilization planning, troop dispositions, force structure, and other concrete issues requiring long lead times to be put in place. Part of the issue today is that the United States and NATO have been so concerned, with good reason, about *means* in NATO that *ends* have been neglected. If SACEUR were directed beforehand that there would be no negotiation so long as a single Pact soldier stood on West German soil, for example, the supreme allied commander might draw certain conclusions regarding the duration and phasing of his defense plans. On the other hand, if NATO left unstated the conditions under which it would seek to terminate an attack, both friend and potential enemy may well regard the outcome of hostilities as negotiable, which is not a strong inspiration for a desperate war.

Not just grand strategy suffers from a lack of definition. The difficulty of putting a "box" around thinking about extended conventional defense stretches to lower echelons of strategy and operations. For instance, logistic constraints are very difficult to pin down. Statements that NATO has only five days' ammunition on hand, or ten, or thirty, admit to all kinds of questions. (Stockage levels may be too low, but the Alliance would not summarily run out of ammunition on the eleventh day. Instead, commanders would ration their stocks from the first day to stretch out their defense, and ammunition would be shifted within theater from lightly engaged units to heavily engaged ones.) The questions should be: With these reduced stocks, what opportunities are lost and what vulnerabilities are risked? How might the Alliance best use intra-theater airlift within NATO? Where and when do the intersections occur between land and sea power in order to make the best use of strategic mobility around the periphery of the Soviet Union? These answers can be sought by gaming, by study, or by any of many other means, but the essential questions must first be formulated and tested.

THREE CONCLUSIONS

From this short investigation into NATO's conventional possibilities in the mid-1980s against a partially mobilized Warsaw Pact attack, several conclusions emerge. First, provided NATO has a clear view of objectives and makes maximum use of the forces it has available, the Alliance appears to have sufficient conventional forces on hand to blunt an initial assault. If those forces are deployed with speed and forethought, they also might contain subsequent Pact breakthrough attempts and put NATO in a posture, after the initial defense phase, to dominate the battlefield in the crucial period between the arrival and containment of the first and second Soviet strategic echelons. Much remains to be done.

Many variables are assumed here, principally a NATO reaction to Pact mobilization within seven days, the participation of the French, and the successful use of light forces in static defense. On the other hand, the Soviets are given credit for efficient mobilization, the full and enthusiastic participation of their satellites, and for effective operational maneuver.

This study deliberately did not set out to address in detail the possibilities of NATO conventional strategy beyond D+30.

The state of NATO's military posture after the arrival of the second strategic echelon depends on many factors, including the decision by the Soviets on when to move their Category 3 divisions, the success of the Alliance in building up its reserves and logistic stockpiles, and the political cohesion of NATO and the Warsaw Pact.

Second, nonnuclear defense means a whole new relationship between Western arms and strategy and the policies of the Alliance. Deterrence in the Brodian sense of making war unthinkable does not fit well in the context of conventional strategy. The use of nuclear weapons may well be futile, at least so long as strategic weapons are linked to theater and tactical ones. But conventional armies are not weapons of mass destruction; their deterrent value resides in their ability to fight and accomplish definite objectives. Thus deterrence is a derived product of military readiness rather than a direct product of its existence, as with strategic missiles.[2]

Ultimately, the philosophy of nonnuclear deterrence becomes remarkably similar to the Soviet view of the role of military forces, the difference being that NATO military policy will continue to treat nuclear deterrence in the traditional Western perspective, whereas the Soviets—at least explicitly—treat nuclear and conventional forces alike. For this reason, the proper term should be "conventional defense" that contributes to an overall deterrent posture. The impact of this change on Western military thought should be to free military strategists and policymakers from the mental straitjackets now imposed by outdated deterrent theory and to turn to the more traditional role of strategy: success on the battlefield.

This is the third and final conclusion of this study. Serious attention to conventional strategy in Europe begins to turn up a need to define success for NATO in case, for whatever reason, deterrence fails. If the forces and logistic support are on hand, or shortly will be, to enable Europe to defend itself with a moderate degree of confidence without having to use nuclear weapons, then flexible response needs to be supported by a military strategy directed at a military mission; for example, the destruction of Soviet and Warsaw Pact forces west of the Polish-USSR border and the reoccupation of Alliance territory. In short, the Alliance will need to define "winning" for its conventional strategy to be effective, an idea that has not been credible in Europe since the mid-1950s. It is hoped that this will not be misunderstood to mean goals that are politically and militarily infeasible, such as the entry of ground forces into Eastern Europe to liberate the Czechs or Hungarians. There are other military objectives to be set that are more urgent and more feasible which NATO should address. The ability to destroy Pact forces on NATO soil is a good example.

This study does not mean to define those goals, only to point out that they will be necessary to derive, and that, given the scenario outlined herein, there are sufficient military forces to conduct the initial defense and perhaps to execute follow-on tasks as well. The fact that logistically NATO may be too weak at present to undertake extensive operations, or that some forces programmed for the latter part of this decade might be better configured for specific missions, should not deter the Alliance from the identification and adoption of a conventional strategy designed to win a conflict with the Soviet Union. It is generally agreed that the West is superior in raw manpower and resources to the Warsaw Pact. If conventional defense is to be debated, part of the debate has to address the use of that superiority. Strategy should precede force development; it has not always done so, but this is a ripe time to make it right.

It should be remembered that war in Europe is unlikely so long as West and East maintain a credible balance of forces, both nuclear and nonnuclear. The imbalance in conventional forces that has existed since the inception of the Alliance, and which became so serious in the early to mid-1970s, is being corrected slowly by a general NATO concern with its conventional defenses.

The issue at hand is conceptual, not yet the size and kind of forces. The Alliance's conventional forces are, or have the potential shortly to be, capable of extended nonnuclear defense, as this study has argued. It remains for NATO and its member nations to make the necessary strategic studies, proposals, and changes to its defense policies to frustrate Soviet conventional doctrine and to transfer the responsibility for nuclear use to the Soviets. In a larger sense, shifting the question to where it properly belongs—on the potential aggressor—also will allow the Alliance to achieve a greater degree of harmony among its members and between its governments and their peoples, to build the confidence and consensus necessary for the preservation of democratic states, not necessarily European states alone, and to maintain the defense of the West in all the finest meanings of the phrase.

Notes

[1] See Richard Ned Lebow, "The Soviet Offensive in Europe: The Schlieffen Plan Revisited?" *International Security* 9, no. 3 (Spring 1985):44. Lebow's historically based analysis argues that the Soviets' offensive strategy is the fundamental cause of the West's insecurity. He also contends that "an American or NATO commitment to a more offensive doctrine can therefore only have the effect of confirming Soviet opinion as to the rectitude of their own offensive strategy."

[2] There are conventional armies that deliberately have open-ended strategic objectives, such as the Swiss defense forces, whose mission is to make invasion so costly an undertaking that a potential aggressor would think twice about attacking. The Swiss solution only works when the defender can reasonably expect some aid from friendly states—or at least from the enemy's enemy—and when his homeland has a relatively low value in resources or geopolitical position. Needless to say, NATO has neither big friends nor isolated geography, but there is an uncomfortable similarity between Swiss and current NATO strategic thinking.

Selected Bibliography

Alford, Jonathan. "Perspectives on Strategy." In John D. Steinbruner and Leon V. Segal, eds., *Alliance Security and the No-First-Use Question.* Washington, DC: Brookings Institution, 1983.
Association of the U.S. Army. *Army Green Book, 1983–84: Status Report on Landpower* 33, no. 10 (1983).
Beard, Robin. "Agenda for Defense: A Congressional Perspective." *Strategic Review* 9, no. 1 (Winter 1981).
Berger, Peter J. "The Course of French Defense Policy." *Parameters* 22, no. 3 (September 1982).
Berman, Robert P., and Baker, John C. *Soviet Strategic Forces: Requirements and Responses.* Washington, DC: Brookings Institution, 1982.
Betts, Richard K. *Surprise Attack.* Washington, DC: Brookings Institution, 1982.
———. "Surprise Attack: NATO's Political Vulnerability." *International Security* 5, no. 4 (Spring 1981).
Bonds, Ray, ed. *The U.S. War Machine.* New York: Crown, 1978.
Boyd, John R. "Patterns of Conflict." Briefing prepared on tempo of warfare. September 1981.
Bracken, Paul. "The NATO Defense Problem." *Orbis* 27, no. 1 (Spring 1983).
Brodie, Bernard, ed. *The Absolute Weapon: Atomic Power and World Order.* New York: Harcourt, Brace, 1946.
Canby, Steven L. "Dampening Nuclear Counterforce Incentives: Correcting NATO's Inferiority in Conventional Military Strength." *Orbis* 19, no. 1 (Spring 1975).
Carnesale, Albert et al. (the Harvard Nuclear Study Group). *Living with Nuclear Weapons.* New York: Bantam, 1983.
Churchill, Winston S. *Their Finest Hour.* Boston: Houghton Mifflin, 1949.
Clausewitz, Carl von. *On War.* Reprint ed. Princeton, NJ: Princeton University Press, 1976.
Clawson, Robert W., and Kaplan, Lawrence S., eds. *The Warsaw Pact: Political Purpose & Military Means.* Wilmington, DE: Scholarly Resources, 1982.
Coffey, Kenneth J. *Manpower for Military Mobilization.* Washington, DC: American Enterprise Institute, 1978.

Collins, John M. *Grand Strategy*. Annapolis, MD: Naval Institute Press, 1973.
———. *U.S.-Soviet Military Balance, 1960–1980*. Washington, DC: McGraw-Hill, 1980.
Congressional Budget Office. *Army Ground Combat Modernization in the 1980s—Potential Costs and Effects for NATO*. Washington, DC: Government Printing Office, 1982.
Corbett, Julian. *Some Principles of Maritime Strategy*. London: Longmans, Green, 1918.
Corcoran, Edward A. *Evolution of European Defense in the 1980s*. Carlisle Barracks, PA: U.S. Army War College, 1981.
Cordesman, Anthony J. "The NATO Central Region and the Balance of Uncertainty." *Armed Forces Journal* 120, no. 12 (July 1983).
Department of the Army. *FM 100-5, Operations*. Washington, DC: Government Printing Office, 1976.
———. *FM 100-5, Operations*. Washington, DC: Government Printing Office, 1982.
———. "Land Power in Transition." In *Posture of the Army and Department of the Army Budget Estimates for Fiscal Year 1984*. Washington, DC: Department of the Army, 1983.
Deputy Chief of Staff for Intelligence. *Soviet Army Operations*. Washington, DC: Department of the Army, 1978.
———. *The U.S. Army Light Infantry Division*. Washington, DC: Department of the Army, 1984.
DeSeversky, Alexander. *Air Power: Key to Survival*. New York: Simon and Schuster, 1950.
Dogherty, Russel. "Concepts and Capabilities." In Kenneth Rush and Brent Scowcroft, eds., *Strengthening Deterrence: NATO and the Credibility of Western Defense in the 1980s*. Cambridge, MA: Ballinger, 1981.
Donnelly, C. N. "The Soviet Operational Maneuver Group—A New Challenge for NATO." *International Defense Review* 15, no. 9 (September 1982).
Douhet, Giulio. *The Command of the Air*. 1921; reprint ed., New York: Coward, McCann, 1942.
Dunn, Keith A., and Staudenmaier, William O. *Alternative Military Strategies for the Future*. Boulder, CO: Westview Press, 1984.
———. *Military Strategy in Transition: Defense and Deterrence in the 1980s*. Carlisle Barracks, PA: U.S. Army War College, 1984.
———. *Strategic Implications of the Continental-Maritime Debate*. New York: Praeger, 1984.
———. "Strategy for Survival." *Foreign Policy*, no. 52 (Fall 1983).
Dupuy, Trevor N. *A Genius for War: The German Army and General Staff, 1807–1945*. Englewood Cliffs, NJ: Prentice-Hall, 1977.
———. "The Soviet Second Echelon: Is This a Red Herring?" *Armed Forces Journal* 119, no. 12 (August 1982).
Dyson, Freeman. *Weapons and Hope*. New York: Harper and Row, 1984.

Dziak, John J. *Soviet Perceptions of Military Doctrine and Military Power: The Interaction of Theory and Practice.* New York: Crane, Russak, 1981.
English, Robert. "Eastern Europe's Doves." *Foreign Policy,* no. 56 (Fall 1984).
Enthoven, Alain C., and Smith, K. Wayne. *How Much Is Enough?* New York: Harper, 1971.
European Security Study. *Strengthening Conventional Deterrence in Europe.* New York: St. Martin's Press, 1983.
Evangelista, Matthew A. "Stalin's Postwar Army Reappraised." *International Security* 7, no. 3 (Winter 1982–83).
Federal Minister of Defense. *White Paper 1979: The Security of the Federal Republic of Germany and the Development of Federal Armed Forces.* Bonn: Ministry of Defense, 1979.
———. *White Paper 1983: The Security of the Federal Republic of Germany and the Development of Federal Armed Forces.* Bonn: Ministry of Defense, 1983.
Freeman, Waldo D. *NATO Central Region Forward Defense: Correcting the Force-Strategy Mismatch.* Washington, DC: National Defense University, 1981.
Ginsburgh, Robert N. "The United States Air Force." In Ray Bonds, ed., *The U.S. War Machine.* New York: Crown, 1978.
Gorshkov, S. G. *The Sea Power of the State.* Russian edition copyrighted by *Voyenizat.* Translation copyrighted by Pergamon Press, 1979. Reprinted by Naval Institute Press, Annapolis, MD.
Gray, Colin S. *American Military Space Policy.* Cambridge, MA: ABT, 1982.
———. *The Geopolitics of the Nuclear Era.* New York: Crane, Russak, 1977.
Herspring, Dale A., and Volgyes, Ivan. "Political Reliability in the Eastern European Warsaw Pact Armies." *Armed Forces and Society* 6, no. 3 (Winter 1980).
Hollingsworth, James F. "Understanding the Conventional Umbrella." *Armed Forces Journal* 121, no. 7 (February 1984).
Huntington, Samuel P. "Conventional Deterrence and Conventional Retaliation in Europe." *International Security* 8, no. 3 (Winter 1983–84).
———. *The Strategic Imperative.* Cambridge, MA: Ballinger, 1982.
Ikle, Fred C. *Every War Must End.* New York: Columbia University Press, 1971.
International Institute for Strategic Studies. *Defense and Consensus* (Adelphi Papers #182). London: IISS, 1983.
———. *The Military Balance, 1983–1984.* London: IISS, 1983.
———. *The Military Balance, 1984–1985.* London: IISS, 1984.
Kaplan, Lawrence S., ed. *NATO and the Policy of Containment.* Lexington, MA: D. C. Heath, 1968.
Kaplan, Lawrence S., and Clawson, Robert W., eds. *NATO After Thirty Years.* Wilmington, DE: Scholarly Resources, 1981.
Kelleher, Catherine. "Nuclear-Conventional Tradeoffs: The Debate in Europe." In Keith A. Dunn and William O. Staudenmaier, eds., *Military*

Strategy in Transition: Defense and Deterrence in the 1980s. Carlisle Barracks, PA: U.S. Army War College, 1984.

Kennan, George ("X"). "The Sources of Soviet Conduct." *Foreign Affairs* 25, no. 4 (July 1947).

Killebrew, Robert B. "Has Light Infantry *Really* Had Its Day?" *Army* 29, no. 12 (December 1979).

Kime, Steve F. "The Soviet View of War." *Comparative Strategy* 2, no. 3 (1980).

Kissinger, Henry A. *Nuclear Weapons and Foreign Policy.* New York: Harper and Row, 1957.

———. "A Plan to Reshape NATO." *Time* 123, no. 10 (5 March 1984).

Komer, Robert W. "Is Conventional Defense of Europe Feasible?" *Naval War College Review* 35, no. 5 (September–October 1982).

———. "Maritime Strategy Versus Coalition Defense." *Foreign Affairs* 60, no. 5 (Summer 1982).

———. "Treating NATO's Self-Inflicted Wound." *Foreign Policy* 13 (1973–74).

Korb, Lawrence J. "The Major Elements of Force Mix Decisions." *Defense '84* (April 1984).

Korbonski, Andrzej. "The Warsaw Treaty After Twenty-Five Years: An Entangling Alliance or an Empty Shell?" In Robert W. Clawson and Lawrence S. Kaplan, eds., *The Warsaw Pact: Political Purpose & Military Means.* Wilmington, DE: Scholarly Resources, 1982.

Lebow, Richard Ned. "The Soviet Offensive in Europe: The Schlieffen Plan Revisited?" *International Security* 9, no. 3 (Spring 1985).

Leebart, Derek, ed. *Soviet Military Thinking.* Boston: George Allen and Unwin, 1981.

Leites, Nathan. "The Soviet Style of War." In Derek Leebart, ed., *Soviet Military Thinking.* Boston: George Allen and Unwin, 1981.

Lellouche, Pierre. "France and the Euromissiles." *Foreign Affairs* 62, no. 2 (Winter 1983–84).

Luttwak, Edward N. *The Grand Strategy of the Soviet Union.* New York: St. Martin's Press, 1983.

Mackinder, Halford. *The Geographical Pivot of History.* London: Royal Geographic Society, 1951.

McNamara, Robert S. "The Military Role of Nuclear Weapons." *Foreign Affairs* 62, no. 1 (Fall 1983).

Mako, William P. *U.S. Ground Forces and the Defense of Central Europe.* Washington, DC: Brookings Institution, 1983.

Mearsheimer, John J. "Why the Soviets Can't Win Quickly in Central Europe." *International Security* 17, no. 1 (Summer 1982).

Middleton, Drew. "For U.S. Army, A New Kind of Infantry Division." *New York Times,* 19 February 1984.

Moreton, Edwina, and Segal, Gerald, eds. *Soviet Strategy Toward Western Europe.* London: George Allen and Unwin, 1984.

North Atlantic Treaty Organization. *NATO and the Warsaw Pact: Force Comparisons*. Brussels, 1984.

Novak, Michael. "Moral Clarity in the Nuclear Age." *National Review* 35, no. 6 (April 1983).

Ørvik, Nils. "A Defence Doctrine for Canada." *Orbis* 27, no. 1 (Spring 1983).

Osgood, Robert. *Containment, Soviet Behavior and Grand Strategy*. Berkeley, CA: Institute of International Studies, 1981.

Petersen, Nikolaj. "Alliance Policies of the Smaller NATO Countries." In Lawrence S. Kaplan and Robert W. Clawson, eds., *NATO After Thirty Years*. Wilmington, DE: Scholarly Resources, 1981.

Posen, Barry. "Competing Views of the Central Region Conventional Balance." In Keith A. Dunn and William O. Staudenmaier, eds., *Alternative Military Strategies for the Future*. Boulder, CO: Westview Press, 1984.

Puscheck, Herbert C. "Selective Service Registrations: Success or Failure?" *Armed Forces and Society* 10, no. 1 (Fall 1983).

Record, Jeffrey. "The Europeanization of NATO: A Restructured Commitment for the 1980s." *Air University Review* 33, no. 6 (September–October 1982).

———. "Is Europe Defensible?" *Baltimore Sun*, 19 April 1984.

———. *NATO's Theater Nuclear Force Modernization Program: The Real Issues*. Cambridge, MA: Institute for Foreign Policy Analysis, 1981.

———. *Sizing Up the Soviet Army*. Washington, DC: Brookings Institution, 1975.

Record, Jeffrey, and Hanks, Robert J. *U.S. Strategy at the Crossroads: Two Views*. Cambridge, MA: Institute for Foreign Policy Analysis, 1982.

Reisz, John B. "Rear Area Combat Operations." *Military Review* 50, no. 12 (December 1979).

Ropp, Theodore. *War in the Modern World*. New York: Macmillan, 1959.

Ross, Steven T. "French Defense Policy." *Naval War College Review* 36, no. 3 (May–June 1983).

Rush, Kenneth, and Scowcroft, Brent, eds. *Strengthening Deterrence: NATO and the Credibility of Western Defense in the 1980s*. Cambridge, MA: Ballinger, 1981.

Sabrosky, Alan Ned. "America in NATO: The Conventional Delusion." *Orbis* 25, no. 2 (Summer 1981).

Samuel, Wolfgang W. E. "The Impossible Task—Defense Without Relevant Strategy." *Air University Review* 31, no. 3 (March–April 1980).

Savkin, V. Y. *The Basic Principles of Operational Art and Tactics*. Moscow, 1972. Translated by U.S. Air Force. Washington, DC: Government Printing Office.

Schemmer, Benjamin F. "NATO's New Strategic Plan: Forward, but Strike Deep." *Armed Forces Journal* 120, no. 3 (November 1982).

———. "TacAir." *Armed Forces Journal* 120, no. 5 (January 1983).

———. "We Can Count on Our Allies; I'm Not Sure the Warsaw Pact Can

Count on Theirs." Interview with General Charles A. Gabriel, USAF. In *Armed Forces Journal* 119, no. 5 (January 1982).

———. "Will NATO's C³/EM/I Systems Let Its 'Strike Deep' Strategy Work?" *Armed Forces Journal* 119, no. 5 (January 1982).

Scott, Harriet Fast, and Fast, William F. *The Armed Forces of the USSR*. Boulder, CO: Westview Press, 1981.

———. *The Soviet Art of War*. Boulder, CO: Westview Press, 1982.

———. *The Soviet Control Structure: Capabilities for Wartime Survival*. New York: Crane, Russak, 1983.

Simis, Konstantin. "An Officer and a Crook: Ripping Off the Red Army." *Washington Post* (weekly edition), 23 January 1984.

Slessor, John. *Strategy for the West*. New York: William Morrow and Sons, 1954.

Sokolovsky, Marshal V. D. *Military Strategy*. New York: Praeger, 1963.

Spykman, Nicholas J. *The Geography of the Peace*. New York: Harcourt, Brace, 1944.

Staudenmaier, William O. "One if by Land, Two if by Sea: The Continental-Maritime Debate." *Army* 33, no. 1 (January 1983).

Steinbruner, John D., and Segal, Leon V., eds. *Alliance Security: NATO and the No-First-Use Question*. Washington, DC: Brookings Institution, 1983.

Stratmann, K. Peter. "Prospective Tasks and Capabilities Required for NATO's Conventional Forces." In European Security Study, *Strengthening Conventional Deterrence in Europe*. New York: St. Martin's Press, 1983.

Suvorov, Viktor. *Inside the Soviet Army*. New York: Macmillan, 1983.

Tuchman, Barbara. *The Guns of August*. New York: Macmillan, 1962.

Turner, Stansfield, and Thibault, George. "Preparing for the Unexpected: The Need for a New Military Strategy." *Foreign Affairs* 61, no. 1 (Fall 1982).

U.S. Army War College Strategic Studies Institute. *NATO Defense Posture in an Environment of Strategic Parity and Precision Weaponry*. Carlisle Barracks, PA: U.S. Army War College, 1976.

Vigor, P. H. *Soviet Blitzkrieg Theory*. New York: St. Martin's Press, 1983.

Von Mellenthin, F. W., Stolfi, R. H. S., and Sobik, E. *NATO Under Attack*. Durham, NC: Duke University Press, 1984.

Weigley, Russell F. *The American Way of War*. Bloomington: Indiana University Press, 1973.

Weinberger, Caspar W. *Annual Report to the Congress, Fiscal Year 1984*. Washington, DC: Government Printing Office, 1983.

———. "Seeking a Consensus for the Common Defense." *Defense '82* (December 1982).

Wickham, John A., Jr. "Continuity and Change: Tempering Army of '80s." In AUSA, *Army Green Book 1983–84* 33, no. 10 (1983).

———. "Reinforcing and Strengthening the Conventional Defense." *NATO's Sixteen Nations*, Special No. 1, vol. 28, no. 5 (1983).

Index

Acheson, Dean, 2–3
Afghanistan, 30, 57, 66–67, 75
"Airland Battle," 31, 34, 36
Alaskan 207th Infantry Group, 33
Albania, 48, 75
Allied Air Forces Central Europe, 35
Allied Forces of Central Europe (AFCENT), 109, 131, 133–34, 136–37
Amsterdam, 21
Angola, 30
Antisubmarine warfare (ASW), 29
Antwerp, 21, 24
Arab-Israeli War (1973), 28
Austria, 21, 38, 40

Ballistic missiles, 36, 41
Baltic Fleet (USSR), 75, 129
Baltic military district, 94, 97–98, 109
Bavaria, 118, 120
Bay of Biscay, 21
Bayreuth, 21–22
Beard, Robin, 30
Beirut, 17
Belgium, 40, 44–45, 104
Belorussian military district, 89, 94, 97–98, 109
Berlin, 22
Betts, Richard, 93–94
Big Four, 115
Black Sea Fleet (USSR), 48, 75, 129–30
Blitzkrieg strategy, 100
Bosporus, 48, 75
Bremen, 21
Bremerhaven, 24, 40, 121
Brodie, Bernard, 1, 10, 60, 145
Brookings Institution, 50–51
Brown, Harold, 12
Brussels, 21
Bulgaria, 47–48, 77

Canada, 3, 40, 43, 45, 130, 138; Canadian Brigade Group, 109
Canby, Steven, 131
Carpathian military district, 97–98, 109
Carter, Jimmy, 30
Center Region, 127
Central Army Group (CENTAG), 40, 109, 118, 120, 126, 132
Central Group (Czechoslovakia), 70
Central Strategic Reserve, 98
Centurion battle tank, 46
Chad, 17
Challenger battle tank, 41
Chieftain battle tank, 41
China, 66, 80, 87, 110
Churchill, Winston, 130
Clausewitz, Carl von, 58, 61, 80
Coburg, 21
Collins, John, 13
"Combat aircraft," 38
Combined Arms Armies, 70
Commander, Allied Forces Central Europe (ComAFCENT), 40, 132–33
Commander, Allied Forces Northern Europe (ComAFNORTH), 38
Command style, 48–50
Congressional Budget Office (US), 99, 116
Consolidation phase of war, 116
Cordesman, Anthony, 88
Crimean War, 72
Czechoslovakia, 21, 116, 120, 146; and NATO, 38, 40; Soviet invasion of, 58, 67–69, 93; and Warsaw Pact, 76–77

Defense Planning Committee (DPC), 95–96
Denmark, 6, 21, 45–46, 75, 102–03, 134; Army Home Guard, 46;

155

Denmark (*cont.*)
  Augmentation Force, 46; Field Army Reserve, 46; Regional Defense Force, 46
Department of Defense (US), 125, 131

Eastern Europe, 9, 76–77, 90, 98, 121, 142
East Germany (German Democratic Republic), 21–22, 66, 76–77, 100. *See also* Intra-German border
Eisenhower administration, 4
Ethiopia, 75
Europe, 115–16, 141
European Security Study, 7

Far Eastern theater, 70, 110
Federal Republic of Germany. *See* West Germany
Fischer, Robert, 13
Flexible response, 3, 5, 26
FM 100-5, Operations (US Army manual), 49
"Follow-On Forces Attack" (FOFA), 31
France, 6, 66, 100, 102, 114, 117, 121, 138; armed forces, 41–43, 90–91; command style of, 50; First French Army, 109; and Germany, 130; manpower, 12; mechanized divisions, 90–91; as member of Big Four, 115; and NATO, 11, 22–24, 96, 117–18, 121–22, 144; navy, 43; and Poland, 77; Rapid Action Force, 42, 138; Second Corps, 118; and the Third World, 16–17; and United States, 22, 118; and view of flexible response, 5
Frankfurt, 22
Frunze Military Academy (USSR), 58
Fulda Gap, 22, 104

Gdansk, 21
German Democratic Republic. *See* East Germany
Germany, 66, 68, 130; *see also* East Germany; West Germany
Gorshkov, S. G., 73
Göttingen, 21
Great Britain (United Kingdom), 6, 25, 74, 96, 129–30, 138; armored divisions, 90–91; British Army of the Rhine (BAOR), 41; ground forces, 40–41, 104; I Corps, 126; as member of Big Four, 115; and NATO, 11, 37, 130; and Poland, 77; Royal Air Force, 41; Royal Navy, 41, 43; and Soviet Union, 72; and the Third World, 17; United Kingdom Mobile Force, 41
Great Patriotic War, 55
Greece, 37, 47–48, 130
Greenland, 74
Greenland-Iceland-United Kingdom (G-I-UK) Gap, 129–30
Group of Soviet Forces, Germany (GSFG), 70, 88
Guderian, Heinz, 66

Hamburg, 21, 38
Harrier aircraft, 41
Harvard Nuclear Study Group, 7
Hitler, Adolf, 68
Hof Corridor, 22, 104
Hollingsworth, James, 11
"Horizontal escalation" concept, 134
Horn of Africa, 30
Hungary, 76–77, 146
Huntington, Samuel, 8, 9

Iberia, 21
Iceland, 37, 74, 129–30
Industrial Revolution, 56
Initial defense phase of war, 115
Intra-German border (IGB), 6, 21, 68, 96, 102, 121, 126; and Federal Republic of Germany, 35, 38; and France, 24; and NATO, 98; and Netherlands, 95
Iranian revolution, 30
Iraq, 48
Iron Curtain, 25, 113
Italy, 37, 46

Japan, 27

Kennedy, John F., 5
Kiev, 48, 89
Kissinger, Henry, 1; *Nuclear Weapons and Foreign Policy*, 4–5
Komer, Robert, 7–9, 127
Korbonski, Andrzej, 75
Korea, 3, 27
Korean War, 34

Lambeth, Benjamin, 93

Lance missile, 41
Latin America, 27, 60
Leipzig, 22
Leites, Nathan, 61
Lenin, Vladimir Ilyich, 12, 57, 61
Leopard I battle tank, 45
Leopard II battle tank, 43, 46
Lines of communication (LOC), 24, 98, 118, 120–23
Lisbon conference (1952), 4
Low Countries, 22, 121
Lübeck, 21
Luttwak, Edward, 56, 58
Luxembourg, 40

Mackinder, Sir Halford, 72
Marder armored-fighting vehicle, 43
Marine amphibious brigade (MAB), 31, 138–39
Marshall Plan (1947), 3
Marx, Karl, 55
Massive retaliation, 2, 4–5, 26
McNamara, Robert S., 5
M-day, 88, 98–99, 102, 136
Mellenthin, F. W. von, 57, 62
Middle East, 17, 99
Middleton, Drew, 125
Military Balance list, 38
Mobilization, 14–16, 87–91, 94, 115
"Mobilization curve," 15
Moltke, Helmuth von, 15
MX missile, 35

Netherlands, 37, 46–47, 104
North Atlantic Treaty Organization (NATO), 26, 70, 88, 90, 92, 99, 115–17, 132; air power, 35–36; armed forces, 50; and Belgium, 44–45; and continental defense, 7–8; and conventional defense, 1; and Czechoslovakia, 38, 40; defense policy, 2, 114; defense spending, 11–12; and flexible response, 5–7, 134; force structure, 8; and France, 22–24, 42, 96, 117–18, 121–22, 144; and Great Britain, 11, 37, 130; and Lisbon conference, 4; manpower, 13–14; and massive retaliation, 2–5; and MC document 14/2, 4; and MC document 14/3, 5; military balance, 78–80; mobilization, 14–16, 94, 123–25; options, 94–97; sensitivity, 141; and SLOCs, 130; "Sovietizing" of, 9; strategies, 86, 125, 143–45; superiority, 102; surveillance systems, 13–14; and United States, 27, 95, 126, 129; and Warsaw Pact, 26, 115–16; and West Germany, 43–44
Northern Army Group (NORTHAG), 40, 96, 104, 109, 118, 132
Northern flank, 47
Northern Fleet (USSR), 14, 129
Northern Group (Poland), 70
North German Plain, 6, 22, 40, 91, 103–04, 107, 118, 126, 134
North Korea, 3
Norway, 31, 34, 47, 75, 130, 138; Army Home Guard, 47
NSC-68 (US policy paper, 1950), 3
Nuclear deterrence, 1–2, 6, 85, 97, 141
Nuclear-powered ballistic missile submarine (SSBN) fleet (USSR), 73, 74–75
Nuclear weapons, 6, 29, 41, 98, 110, 115, 141, 145

Odessa, 48
Operational Maneuver Groups (OMB), 132
"Operational reserve," 132
Osgood, Robert, 4

Pacific Fleet (USSR), 75, 129
Paris, 22
Passau, 21
Persian Gulf, 27, 137–38
Phantom aircraft, 41
Pluton tactical nuclear missile, 41
Poland, 22, 76–77, 116
Posen, Barry, 107–08
Prepositioned Overseas Materiel Configured in Unit Sets (POMCUS), 31–32, 99, 124–25, 132
Prussia, 25

Quick Reaction Force (QRF), 42

Radford, Arthur, 4
Rapid Deployment Forces, 29–30, 33, 99, 137–38
Ready Reserve Fleet (US), 31
Record, Jeffrey, 9, 89

Reforger exercises, 16, 124
Remotely piloted vehicles (RPV), 36
Reservists, 25–26
"Revolutionary strategy," 59
Rogers, Bernard, 7–8, 11
Rokossovskiy, Konstantin, 76
Romania, 48, 76–77
Rotterdam, 24

Samuel, Wolfgang, 114
Saxe, Hermann Maurice de, 48–49
Scandinavia, 74
Schleswig-Holstein, 40, 45
Sea lines of communication (SLOC), 74, 130, 139
Sinnrich, Richard, 9
Southern flank, 47
Southern Group (Hungary), 70
Southern theater, 70
Southwest Asia, 31
South Yemen, 75
Sovietizing, 9
Soviet Union (USSR, Russia), 1, 8, 10, 21, 99, 142–43; armed forces, 78, 90–91; command style of, 57, 61–63, 113; Communist Revolution, 55; conventional doctrine, 66; and conventional superiority, 3–4; and Czechoslovakia, 58, 67–69, 93; and Deep Attack, 66; defense spending, 11–12; echelonment doctrine, 63–64; economic growth, 59–60; Field Army, 65; Frontal Aviation, 70; General Staff, 61, 70, 87–88, 97–98; Ground Forces, 70–71, 73, 93; High Command, 97, 109; invasion of Afghanistan, 30; Khrushchev period in, 59; Main Military Council of the Defense Ministry, 70; manpower, 13, 79; military branches, 70; military doctrine, 115, 141; military history, 56–58; military organization, 70–75; military power, 59–60; missile force, 6; mobilization of, 30, 72, 87–91, 94–95, 123, 135; motorized divisions, 90–91; National Air Defense Troops (Voyska PVO), 70; and NATO, 58, 65–66; naval forces, 129–30; offensive doctrine, 62–63; operational doctrine, 60–61, 66, 107; operational maneuver groups (OMG), 65, 80; Politburo, 58; Red Army, 21, 57, 79, 107; reservists, 25; "revolutionary strategy," 59; sea power, 73–74; Second Guards Tank Army, 104; *Spitznaz* units, 66; Strategic Rocket Forces, 70; strategy of, 55–60, 67–70; and surprise attack option, 91–94; technology, 28; Third Shock Army, 104; and United States, 55, 86; view of nuclear war, 86–87; and Warsaw Pact, 75–78, 86, 123, 126, 143; and World War II, 65
Spain, 37
Spykman, Nicholas, 73
Stalin, Joseph, 68, 76
Stratmann, Peter, 131
Supreme Allied Commander Europe (SACEUR), 7, 116–18, 120, 122, 143; reserve, 131–39
Supreme Headquarters, Allied Powers Europe (1950), 4
Surprise attack option, 91–94
Suvorov, Viktor, 57–58, 62, 64
Sweden, 75
Syria, 48, 60

Theaters of military operations (TVD), 70
Thibault, George, 9
Third World, 9, 16, 60
"Titanic coincidence," 93
Toronado aircraft, 41
Trotsky, Leon, 57
Truman administration, 3
Turkey, 37, 47–48, 130, 133
Turner, Stansfield, 9

United Kingdom. See Great Britain
United States, 17, 70, 99, 121; Air Force, 31, 34–35, 108, 124; air power, 34–38; armored divisions, 90–91; Army, 28–29, 31, 62, 120, 132, 138; Civil Reserve Air Fleet, 31–32, 124–25; command style of, 49; and flexible response, 5–7; and France, 22, 118; Individual Ready Reserves (IRR), 33; Joint Chiefs of Staff, 4; land forces, 32–33, 136; light forces, 125–28; line of communication, 92; manpower, 27–28; Marine Corps, 34, 130; and massive retaliation, 2–5; mechanized divisions, 90–91; as member of Big Four, 115;

Merchant Marine, 29; military obligations, 27; mobilization of, 15, 29, 30, 123, 125; National Guard, 27, 33, 95; and NATO, 27, 95, 126, 129; naval power, 9, 36–37, 129; Navy, 34, 129; and nuclear superiority, 3; and out-of-area interests, 9; peacetime draft, 27, 33; and Poland, 77; reservists, 25–26; and Soviet Union, 55, 86; Strategic Air Command, 4, 60; Tactical Air Command, 37–38; and West Germany, 44

Vietnam, 75–76
Vietnam War, 26–27, 34
Vigor, P. H., 68–69, 91–92
Vladivostok, 75
VSTOL aircraft carriers, 75

Wales, 43
Warsaw Pact, 23, 42, 92, 132, 144–45; armed forces, 50, 71; blitzkrieg strategy, 100; and Czechoslovakia, 76–77; manpower, 13–14; military balance, 12, 78–80; mobilization of, 14–16, 88–90, 94, 97–98; and NATO, 26, 115–16; origins of, 75–76; and Soviet Union, 75–78, 86, 123, 126, 143; strategies of, 86; and United States, 32
Weimar, 22
Western Europe, 2–3, 22, 25–26, 113, 142
Western theater, 70
West Germany (Federal Republic of Germany), 5, 6, 7, 11, 21, 23, 35, 37, 41, 99, 102, 125–26, 143; armed forces, 43–44; armored divisions, 90–91; construction industry, 129; Field Army, 25, 43; mechanized divisions, 90–91; as member of Big Four, 115; mobilization of, 15; Naval Air Arm, 44; Tactical Command, 44; Territorial Army, 13, 25, 43–44, 95, 104, 108, 128; and United States, 44; White Paper on Defense (1979), 23; *see also* Intra-German border
Wilhelm, kaiser of Germany, 15
Wolfsburg, 21

Yugoslavia, 48